OCEAN BIRD

They that go down to the sea in ships: and
 occupy their business in great waters;
These men see the works of the Lord: and
 his wonders in the deep.

      – Book of Common Prayer

Ocean Bird

7000 Miles in a Trimaran

Ralph Stephenson

A Deirdre McDonald Book
Bellew Publishing
London

First published in 1993
by Deirdre McDonald Books
128 Lower Richmond Rd
London SW15 1LN

Copyright © Ralph Stephenson 1993

The right of Ralph Stephenson to be identified as the author of this Work has been asserted by him in accordance with the Copyright, Design and Patents Act 1988

All rights reserved

ISBN 1 85725 076 1

Phototypeset by Intype, London
Printed and bound in Great Britain by
Hartnolls Ltd

Contents

Preface		vii
Introduction: Whys and Wherefores		ix
	PART ONE: PREPARATION	1
1	Off with the Old	3
2	On with the New	9
3	Best Buy	16
4	'Men are not measured by Inches'	24
5	Fitting Out	31
6	Down the Channel	38
7	A Needle to an Anchor	45
	PART TWO: THE CRUISE	55
8	The Harbour Cleared	57
9	Las Palmas	71
10	Second Wind	78
11	Cape Verde and Beyond	85
12	In the Doldrums	93
13	Across the Line	99
14	Beyond the South-East Trades	106
15	Trouble at Sea	112
16	More Trouble	120
17	Journey's End	128
18	At the Cape	132
	Epilogue: Tying Rope-Ends	141
	Appendix 1 Stores and Equipment Carried	143
	Appendix 2 Technical Note	145

Preface

This account of a sea voyage from Lymington in Hampshire to Cape Town in an Ocean Bird trimaran can be read as a straightforward adventure story, a heart-lifting glimpse of sky and ocean, a three-men-in-a-boatish jaunt, a model of how-to-do-it-yourself, or a warning of how-not-to. It also has a period flavour, having been written well after the event, once I had retired from a busy life ashore. To adapt Wordsworth: 'Emotion [or action] recollected in tranquillity.'

In this space-and-time-travelling age, it is a relief to turn to wind power and one may be excused for presenting a time-capsule sailing venture. Voyaging in small boats has changed little, even over the ages. The most important change since our voyage, as shown throughout the book and in Appendix 1, is that prices have increased at least five times. Technically the biggest difference is that now less skill in off-shore navigation is required – that is if one has the money and equipment to get satellite information. (Appendix 2 provides a note on navigational terms for the general reader.)

Many sailing enthusiasts who have never been out of sight of land want to venture further. This account should reassure them that it isn't the most difficult thing in the world; and with common sense isn't the most dangerous either. Armchair sailors can also enjoy the drama with total peace of mind.

London   R.S.
1992

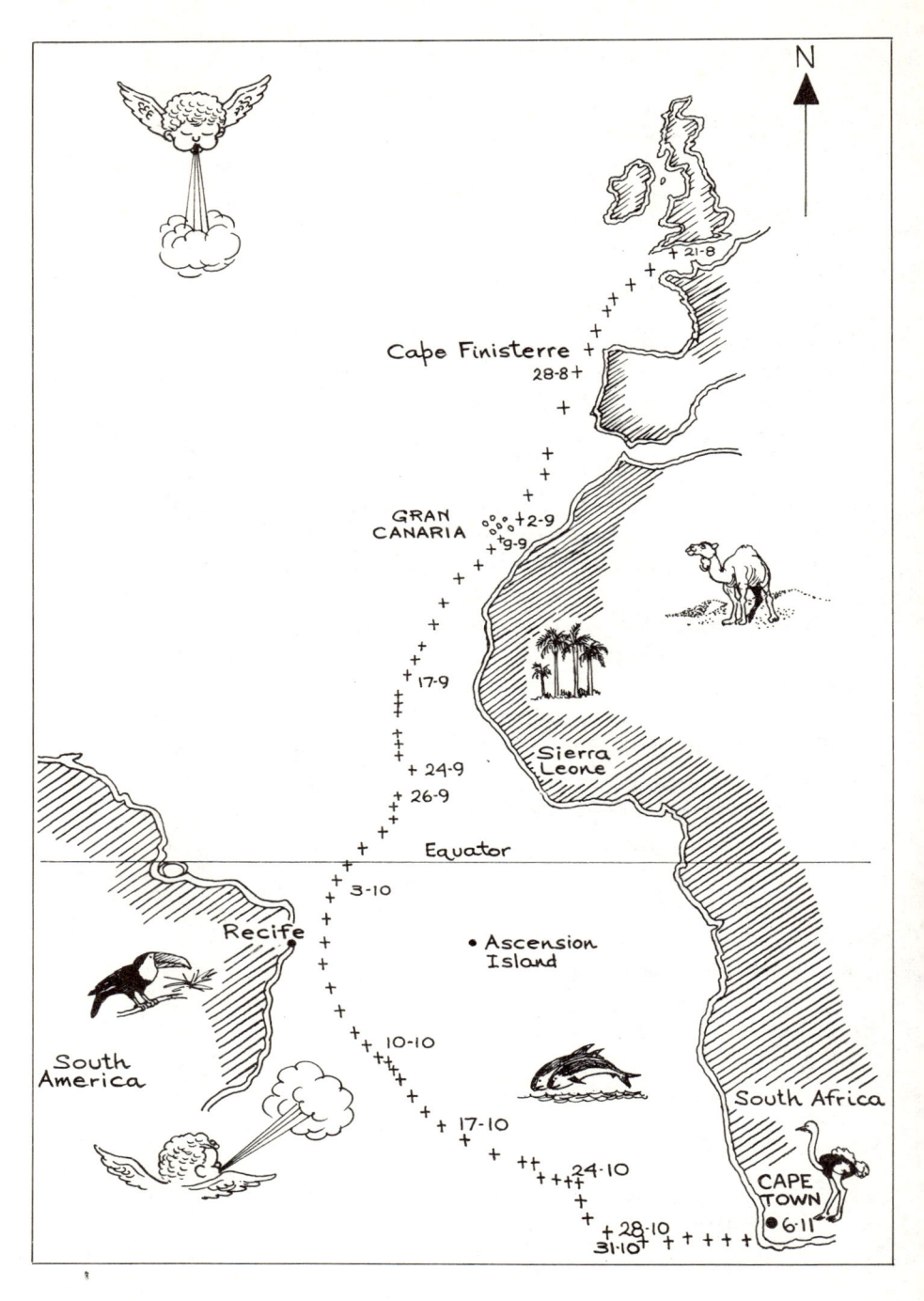

Noon Positions. 21st. August to 6th. November.

Introduction
Whys and Wherefores

I STARTED sailing in Hong Kong, where I had my first job. Yachts were cheap and gave an escape from the teeming crowds of the city. I could camp in the cockpit with a primus stove and a li-lo, buy fish from the passing sam-pan and, anchored in a quiet cove, spend a peaceful week-end often on my own. That came to an end with the war, a short stint on a naval patrol-boat being high-level bombed for four weeks (very regular hours the Jap planes kept – nine to five) and then four years in prison camp. I was lucky, being a lieutenant in the RNVR, to go into an officers' camp of 500 where morale was high, rations low and our treatment, as we learned afterwards, might have been a lot worse.

My next job was in post-war Seychelles, that amoral Island Paradise. 'Four fish for a shilling, four women for a fish' was the crude, sexist saying. On my first day, a departing G.I., met in the hotel, offered me a huge box of several hundred French letters – standard issue. 'I sure don't need them now,' he said.

The only yachts available there were locally built and modelled on old whalers. Round-hulled, clinker-built open boats, carrying a lot of sail for harbour racing at week-ends, they not infrequently capsized. Fortunately they could be righted again and in that mild climate a dip added to the fun. The locals sailing *en famille* usually won, but sometimes they capsized too, and I still have a vivid mental shot of matronly wife, staid husband and assorted kids, all fully clothed (strict church propriety prevailed), floating round their boat intent on rejoining the race.

I got no sailing in my last two jobs abroad. In Ghana (then the Gold Coast) the breakers pounded on the shore and bathing and surfing were the order of the day. In Sierra Leone I was busy with a spear-gun and mask, diving quietly through shoals of fish, mainly enjoying that dazzling other world, but bringing home fish for dinner too.

Then it was back to England. In the 1960s you could still hire a small cabin-cruiser for £25 a week and I went out single-handed from Chichester Harbour along the coast, learning a lot about tides (up till then they had hardly mattered) and going aground in the mud. A friend introduced me to multihulls and eventually I was able to buy my own boat, a catamaran called *Pussy Cat*. She had been built in the north of Sweden. It took me a few hours to fly there and three weeks to sail her back to England. The Swedes who built the boat came with me as far as Brunsbüttel, at the western end of the Kiel Canal, then without warning told me they wanted to go back home for their mid-summer festival. Left alone with a strange boat it took me five days to sail her single-handed across the North Sea. I arrived safely at Sheerness, but I was tired and sleepy and fell into the water as dockhands were helping me tie the boat up.

Coastal cruising, crossings to Holland, Belgium, France and the Channel Islands followed, and a longer cruise round Portugal and Spain, via the Balearics and Cagliari to Malta, then back next season via Sicily, Porto Cervo in Sardinia and across France through the Canal du Midi. These were voyages I did in *Pussy Cat* – with crews of up to 7 or 8. I wrote about her adventures in *5000 Miles in a Catamaran* so need say no more except for a brief note in the next chapter on her career after I had sold her.

Then I looked for a boat suitable for a longer ocean cruise with a smaller crew. I had been born and brought up in New Zealand, left it to wander round the world, and had not been back for nearly forty years. Growing older one cares more and more about roots, and I longed to see the country again, refresh the memories of my youth and look up relatives and friends. My brother, a sheep-farmer, had recently died, my sister was older than I was. It was time I paid the place a visit.

Also I wanted to do a long sea voyage. By then I had been sailing off and on for a good many years, but mostly day-sailing in foreign parts and coastal cruising in European waters. Both historically and technically there is a difference between these cruises and a long ocean voyage. Historically, short passages and coastal journeys were mostly what the ancient and mediaeval sea-goers experienced with their tiny boats and primitive equipment – except for the fabled voyages of the Vikings and the incredible feats of those sea heroes, the Polynesians. In the centuries following Columbus there was ocean voyaging on a different scale, with time at sea counted not by days but by weeks, months and even years. For a small yacht, too, there are technical differences. It is not more dangerous on the open sea. Storms can be as bad near the land where there are more rocks, sand-banks and big ships to run you down. But for coastal sailing you don't need celestial navigation, you can get by with dead reckoning and radio bearings, and the lighthouses are never far over the horizon. You don't say goodbye to the rest of humanity for weeks, you don't have to be so self-contained, so self-reliant.

These were my two aims and it seemed sensible to combine them. However, there is a certain improbability about the feat of 'killing two birds with one stone' and there is the other saying to warn against 'falling between two stools'. In the event I managed to make a long ocean voyage and I got to visit New Zealand. But I didn't manage to sail the whole way. One factor that made it impossible was time. I had retired and I hadn't retired. As a joint venture three of us had taken on a small art cinema in London, appointed ourselves directors, and held periodic board meetings. The cinema jogged undramatically along, and when I asked my co-directors if they would agree to my going on a long ocean cruise lasting three, or at the most four, months if I forwent directors fees, they seemed happy to humour me.

The time might have been long enough. But human estimates are inclined to be optimistic, and it was not only some slow passages on the voyage but the matter of repairs here and in strange ports, that bogged me down. What with the Israeli War, the rail strike, the oil crisis, the three-day week – days stretched into weeks before one could even place an order. The route we chose, down to the Canaries and on to the Cape seemed the most straightforward. I was influenced by Francis Chichester's *Along the Clipper Way* and Whitbread Round-the-World races. If Suez had been open we might have gone that way. Cape Horn was too tough, especially east to west. Though the way through Panama might have given us warmer weather, shorter hops and more favourable winds, I doubt if it would have been quicker, taking into consideration stop-overs in harbour and getting through the Canal. I had never visited South Africa and had heard it was a fascinating and beautiful country.

If I seem to take a long time describing our preparations for the voyage, one reason is that my most enjoyable holidays (those organised and carried out myself) have given as much pleasure in the planning as in the doing – an extension perhaps of Robert Louis Stevenson's 'to travel hopefully is better than to arrive'. As I say later, we had delays and setbacks from start to finish. But on balance how worthwhile and what an experience it turned out to be. Apart from the war, it was in retrospect the adventure of my wandering but fairly comfortable existence. Then there was the sheer pleasure of sailing day after day. Like surfing, skating, skiing, gliding, ballooning, sailing is moving naturally with the elements, far more peaceful and soul-satisfying than moving by mechanical means. Rocketing forward accompanied by the roar of motor-boat, motor-car, motor-bike or jet-plane is quite another rackety experience. Then there was the endless vastness of the sea, the remoteness of its countless inhabitants, the splendour of its cloud mountains. As well as the land the sea has its scenery too. Finally despite any disagreements, there was the easy companionship of co-mates in a common enterprise, an undemanding human relationship that our compartmented modern world sometimes denies us.

Part One
PREPARATION

DAY 8.
SEPTEMBER
15 Saturday

3819 3693
960
59.

Too hot in cabin to sleep well.

Week 37 (258-107)

SEPTEMBER
S 2 9 16 23 30
M 3 10 17 24
T 4 11 18 25
W 5 12 19 26
T 6 13 20 27
F 7 14 21 28
S 1 8 15 22 29

584
694
140

Bar - 1023. Cloud 9510. Very grey.
Watch 65 sec. slow on GMT. at 0800.
Wind — Log at 0800 - 692 miles.
more easterly - force 4/5.
Shower of rain abt 0800.   { Flying fish for breakfast.
Taking hourly tricks at helm.
Again more motion - tiring.   (No morning
0830 - RDF. SaL. bearing   (sight of sun.
243 - Zone say 230.
with 110 mm) puts us   Trying to rain
in log.   21°30' West. 17°40' North
morning sight after all - Sun came out. —
azimuth 98° - Gives comp. ale. 21°42'W.
omlette & flying fish (grilled) for lunch - beer.
Playing chess
Mer. alt - Lat. 17°20'6'(N) with morning
sight b.f. gives Comp. 21°55'!   { Strong but
SAL bearing about 250-255° Compass &   much interference
up to G.W. N°50 (Telegraph)   { Electric log at
Walker log giving trouble.   { miles 3760. 1410
? oiling right place? ——→ · { Walker log. 723
Landbird (swallow) rested on boat.
another small bird came in evening.   very
Wind veering south - on an easy beat now.   light
Self steering with staysail working OK.   sheet 3kts
                                            (to 4 kts)
                                           next
                                           tack

Page from the ship's log. Day 8; 15th. September.

1
OFF WITH THE OLD

According to a saying in sailing circles, 'There are two ecstatic days in a yachtsman's life. One is the day he buys a boat; the other is the day he sells it.' Whatever one may think of such cynicism on a serious subject, there is no doubt that owning a particular boat marks a chapter in one's sailing experience. More than in most recreations, cruising takes its character from the boat, and boats differ in almost every particular. This then is as much an account of a cruising trimaran, as of the long voyage and the three of us who made it.

Cruises in *Pussy Cat*, my previous mistress, had ended successfully. She had stood up to a lot of hard going and we had parted on good terms. But she had led me a dance in some ways, especially where her outboard engine was concerned. It was better for us to part. My last cruise ended in Plymouth and I sold her to an unusual young couple, a South African, whose family farmed orange-groves outside Johannesburg, married to a Polish girl: Johann and Alicja. They had friends in Portugal and planned (it was September) to live on the boat over the winter and then, when they had more experience, sail her down the Portuguese coast and back to South Africa. There was some to-and-froing about payment, and when Johann disappeared by air to Johannesburg, I had qualms about having let them take over the boat before it had been paid for. However, he was simply making some complex manoeuvres to find a legal way through an African forest of exchange control, and he reappeared in a week's time and paid the brokers in full.

Because South Africa had left the Commonwealth, it proved impossible to transfer the British Registry and the brokers gave Johann a photostat copy, the original being returned to me cancelled, like a passport with the corners chopped off. There was a link here between my new boat *Swingaway* and the old one, since the same difficulty arose when I sold *Swingaway* to another South African,

Ron, from Durban. It was also due to the cancelled British Registry that I learned something of *Pussy Cat*'s subsequent history.

Johann and Alicja settled in comfortably for the winter, had two trips across the Channel in the spring, then set off across the Bay of Biscay. They had some hard weather en route, their friends from Portugal dropped out somehow, and though they got the boat safely to Gibraltar, they had by then had enough – or at least Alicja had. It is remarkable that short-handed and having never set foot on a yacht before, they accomplished so much, so quickly. They decided to give up and sell the boat, and the agents rang up and asked if I would like to buy the boat back at a lower price. Also, later again, a much redirected letter reached me which proved to contain an account for mooring fees from the Naval Dockyard at Gib. I disclaimed responsibility, but I had no idea of Johann's whereabouts, and I wondered if poor *Pussy Cat* had been abandoned.

Then in 1975 three years after I had sold her, I had a phone call from a new owner of *Pussy Cat* who had bought her from Johann and had been using her for charter cruises to Normandy and the Channel Islands. He was about to sell her to two ex-fliers turned sailors whose destination was the Seychelles Islands in the Indian Ocean via the newly reopened Suez Canal. It would be important for them to have British Registry going through the Canal, and as I was the last registered owner, my signature was necessary on the now-to-be-uncancelled certificate. I like to think of *Pussy Cat* being one of the first yachts through the Canal and eventually sunning herself amid the coral reefs of those remote islands where I had once sailed.

Pussy Cat had her faults. The main cabin floors were two or three feet too low, and the resultant slamming when going into a head sea was hardly compensated for by the unusual feature that one could stand upright *on* the large double bunks. The watertanks were in the keels and quite inaccessible, so it seemed impossible to eliminate the slight but persistent taste of fibre-glass resin which flavoured the water and gave a peculiar tang to the strongest brew of tea or coffee. Then there were the fin keels which replaced earlier centre-boards. They had the advantage of simplicity, but when going to windward in light airs they were not deep or long enough to prevent the boat making a lot of leeway.

A ketch rig is fine in many ways, but I found the mizzen sail interfered with that *sine qua non* of short-handed voyages – self-steering. I had a horizontal wind-vane self-steering fitted to the starboard hull which worked well when *Pussy Cat* was on the starboard tack and the gear was to windward of the mizzen sail. But on the port tack and the other way about, there was always trouble. One could possibly have rigged up some means of transferring the gear or fitted a second vane, but these drawbacks helped to turn my thoughts to the simplicity of a sloop rig and the convenience of a trimaran's central hull. This again would simplify the engine fitting. I had had endless trouble with the heavy outboard and a central bracket to lower it into the water. It is possible for catamarans to carry twin inboard engines, one in each hull, but it means double expense and double maintenance, hardly justified except for a motor-sailer. There are no such problems with a trimaran or a monohull, and a single engine can be centrally mounted. Finally there were minor annoyances like the loo (an SL 400) that wouldn't pump in water, perhaps because it had been mounted too high, and the electric wiring and badly-sited fuse box that kept corroding.

So I set out with an open mind to look around. I had been sailing nothing but multihulls for four years, but I didn't rule out monohulls. The picture I had in my mind was of a boat suitable for a long cruise, possibly as far as New Zealand. The plan of the cruise is more fully discussed in chapter 4. All I need say here is that I had given up the idea of taking large numbers on charter cruises, so nothing like *Pussy Cat*'s eight berths would be needed. To a large extent I was prepared to fit my plans to the boat. And of course, like all optimistic buyers, I wanted the perfect boat that had no faults, wouldn't give any trouble, was fast, easily handled and all at a bargain price.

First I looked at a couple of monohulls. I drove out to Southend and went out for a trial sail in a 27-foot Jaguar, an American design that had not been very long on the market. Compared to *Pussy Cat* she was a mini to a pantechnicon, and when I stepped on board she heeled over slightly. I must say when we set off down the Roach in a light breeze she bowled along very nicely and handled as easily as a dinghy – sails, steering, engine, the lot. Also she was nicely finished and pretty reasonable in price. I expect one *could* have gone round the world in her – but either single-handed or with a very matey crew.

A couple of weeks later I drove down to Littlehampton and tried out a MacWester, a broader, beefier yacht, very solid and strong but without the pace or manoeuvrability of the Jaguar and more expensive. At the same time there was more living space and stowage. When we got off-shore there was too little wind for her and we had to come back under the engine. This type of yacht is extremely popular (there are other makes which have similar qualities) and is so no doubt with yachtsmen who don't want to break records, preferring something comfortable and really hard-wearing. In its way it is a traditional British product, safe and enduring like certain cars from the Morris 1000 to the Bentley. The nearest thing in the multihull market perhaps, is the Bobcat or its successor the Catalac.

I couldn't make up my mind about either of these boats, and then a third possibility offered itself. My friend Tony had decided to sell his Triune, *Sophie*, a 30-foot trimaran, and set himself the enormous task of building with his own hands a 48-foot trimaran to a Kelsall design. He had hired a space in a warehouse in the Surrey Docks and except when on call in his medical practice, was prepared to spend every weekend for the next umpteen years cutting, screwing, moulding, trueing, assembling and what have you. He had had a buyer for *Sophie*, but somehow the sale fell through and she was on the market again.

This was the first multihull I ever sailed and I was very fond of her. She had been built in Poole in 1966 in the then common construction of marine ply covered with a layer of fibreglass. I had had an extensive cruise in her in 1968 and been out more briefly on several other occcasions. She was well equipped and Tony had looked after her carefully. She was pretty fast, had a very reliable diesel engine, was comfortable in all conditions, and would sleep up to six, at any rate for short cruises. That week-end Tony drove me up to Maylandsea near Maldon in Essex, where *Sophie* was hauled out on a slipway, to have a look at her. There were one or two problems like a leaking water-tank that couldn't be taken out for repair without removing a cross-beam, and a track that was lifting off the deck, but Tony promised to put everything right, we agreed on a price subject to survey, and I thought I had found what I wanted.

But the next week I had a telephone call from the surveyor. He had gone from Burnham to Maylandsea and after a preliminary look decided to telephone me before making a detailed survey.

'I don't think this boat is suitable for your purpose. That is for a long ocean voyage,' he said. 'There are some weaknesses. I rang up to save you the cost of a full survey. If you like I can write briefly and say what I think is wrong, and I'll charge you only my expenses and a nominal fee. But I'll go ahead if you like. It's up to you.'

I wasn't very happy at this news as I wanted to go ahead for every reason, but I gave what seemed the sensible reply: if he thought there were any defects which might make *Sophie* unsafe for a long voyage, then that was all I would want to know.

I got his letter a couple of days later and an account for £15 which was very little compared with the fee for a full survey. He wrote that while the boat would be fine for cross-Channel and coastal cruises probably for many years to come, he thought she was too lightly constructed for a long ocean voyage; that there was evidence of some delamination and weakness where the edges joined at one bow; that some of the stay fittings could be heavier, tracks were screwed instead of bolted to the deck; and so on.

I mention this in detail because it represents a whole stage in the development of multihulls. Boats were deliberately built light, even the weight of each piece of equipment taken on board was carefully gauged, and owners were exhorted to limit their personal baggage. The results in speed and liveliness were remarkable, but durability, especially under the ceaseless strain of weeks at sea, had to suffer. One has to consider the entirely different scale of two kinds of sailing. On a two-week Channel cruise calling at half-a-dozen ports one may cover 200 or so miles, choosing one's weather and sailing often in calm or sheltered waters. The shortest Atlantic crossing will be ten times this distance. It will be twice as far to the West Indies, four times as far to South Africa, round the world one or two hundred times as far – and the boat will be under constant stress and strain. A well-known case of this type of construction giving way occurred in the *Sunday Times* single-handed race round the world. Nigel Tetley in a Piver trimaran was leading the field and on his way back to Southampton when his boat (by no means new when the race started and built of light marine ply and fibreglass) came apart at the seams and sank within a few hours. He had by this time crossed his outward track and made a record at the time of 179 days for the fastest single-handed voyage round the world. But with his boat at the bottom of the sea he lost the race to the slower but solider ketch, *Suhaili*, sailed by Robin Knox-Johnston. And it was only by the grace of God, reading between the lines of his book *Trimaran Solo*, that Tetley was picked up in time by a cargo boat. Piver himself disappeared at sea in 1968 on a cruise down the Californian coast.

Sophie was a lot stronger than the early Piver boats, but tempering rashness with caution, I wasn't disposed to take a chance, even though it was a disappointment. After a preliminary telephone call I sent Tony a copy of the surveyor's letter with a covering note. I am glad to say he sold the boat shortly after and she is still cruising in home waters. Indeed it so happens that she rounded Selsey Bill in a bad storm on the very day (and within two hours of the time) when Edward Heath's yacht *Morning Cloud* was sunk and two of the crew lost. *Sophie* came safely through. Which may be a comment on the surveyor's report – or on the relative safety of monohulls and multihulls – or simply on the luck of the sea.

2
On with the New

On my first cruise in a multihull, in *Sophie* that is, we had spent a day in Dartmouth harbour. While we were lying moored fore-and-aft to buoys opposite the marina, a strange yacht came surging down the river with a fair tide and a beam wind. About 30 feet long, she looked to me at the time like a flying spider. I was unused then even to the idea of a boat half built of steel girders, a floating meccano monster. Since creatures like the extraordinary *Pen Duik IV* (later changed to *Manureva*) have been breaking traditions as well as speed and distance records, we are more used to yachts looking like something out of science fiction. When a local visitor came on board, I asked him about the boat that had passed us.

'Oh that's an Ocean Bird,' he told me. 'A swing-wing trimaran. The floats can be folded in when you come into harbour, so she takes up no more berthing space than a monohull. They build them up river at Totnes.'

Later I became used to seeing Honnor Marine's advertisement in the monthly magazine *Multihull International*: 'No Ocean Bird has ever capsized . . . ever broken apart . . . large protected cockpits and comfortable accommodation . . . sail fast without appreciable heeling or rolling . . . they have proven sea-going ability.' So now that I was again uncommitted and looking for a boat, I thought about an Ocean Bird. It was one of the few multihulls I had not looked at in 1970 before I bought *Pussy Cat*.

I had met Monty, then the editor of *Multihull International* and decided to ask his opinion. As usual he was knowledgeable and helpful. 'You might do worse,' he said, 'I don't suppose there's any such thing as the perfect boat. But owners seem to like them and keep them. They are really well built. You don't see many on the market.'

I said I didn't think I could afford a new boat which was then about £10,000.

'Why don't you get in touch with John Westell at Honnor Marine and ask if he knows of any second-hand boats? If there isn't anything immediately, there might be if you're prepared to wait a few months.'

John Westell, designer for Honnor Marine, was equally helpful when I wrote to him. He wrote back to say that he had been asked to build a new 35-foot boat for an Ocean Bird owner who wanted to change his present 30-footer for something larger. The owner, Ken Cooper, intended to sell his present boat, and John Westell would write and tell him that I was interested. Soon after that I got a letter from Ken who wrote from a country address near Nottingham. The boat was called *Swingaway* and it was berthed in one of the marinas at Lymington, a port I'd only passed through by ferry on the way to Yarmouth in the Isle of Wight. It was out of the water and I could see her at any time at the marina. She had been well looked after and was well equipped, but there were some things he wanted to keep for his new boat. He was asking £6,500. I had got £6,000 for *Pussy Cat* so it was well worth going into further. Ken told me how to get to the marina, where the key was to be found when I got there, and to ask for Dave Orchard at the boat-yard.

Then within a few days and before I had time to get down to Lymington I had another letter. Ken wrote to say he was sorry but he had decided after all not to sell *Swingaway*. His new boat wouldn't be ready in time for next summer, and he didn't want to miss a season's sailing through not having a boat. It looked as though I was going to be cast adrift again, but a possible solution was to suggest some sort of sharing arrangement. So I wrote back putting the idea in a general way, and saying that in any case I wouldn't want to leave England until the end of summer. When we spoke on the phone Ken liked the suggestion and predicted he wouldn't want to use *Swingaway* for more than about six weeks.

By then it was Christmas and it was arranged I would go and have a look at the boat as originally planned in January. Ken was coming to London for the Boat Show and proposed I should join him and his wife together with John Westell for supper at his hotel. The prime purpose of the meeting was for him and John to discuss details of Ken's new Ocean Bird, but there was a lot of conversation about sailing generally, and Ken gave me some details and a picture of *Swingaway*. Further discussion would have to wait until I had seen her.

When I drove down to Lymington it was a bright winter's day, the whole world was drenched in pale lemon sunshine, there was no wind and it was not too cold. In the town I drove through a thriving street market, past well-kept 1930s houses and neat streets, finding myself at the river, which bristled with masts, where the ferry to Yarmouth dwarfed the few hardy small-boat winter sailors, booming at them from time to time to make way in the narrow channel.

I had to turn back as the approach to the marina was the other side of town, down a rural lane with cows in the neighbouring fields. Just inside the yard-gates were the yachts spending the winter out of the water. There were perhaps twenty or thirty of them, mostly supported by legs, on a wide stretch of gravel. They seemed well-ordered and peaceful in the sunshine, waiting as content and reposeful as the cows on the other side of the hedge. *Swingaway* was not far from the entrance and easily identified since she was the only trimaran there out of the water (I saw several later lying in their berths) and the only 'swing-wing' trimaran in the place. Like a bird at rest she was perched comfortably without any props on two crosspieces of timber which went under the main hull, and with her swinging floats tucked like wings into her sides and placed on extra blocks. On the whole with her soft red anti-fouling and white topsides, she had a subdued look, but there was a flamboyant touch about the name painted in large letters along the side of each of the two floats. I drove the car over the gravel and parked alongside the boat, then went to the yard at the entrance to make myself known. They were too busy to be all that interested when I asked for Dave and said I had arranged with Ken Cooper to look over *Swingaway*.

'She's just over there on the hard,' Dave said. 'Help yourself.'

I went back to the boat and after a tour of inspection which established that there was no ladder, scrambled on to one of the floats and thence on board. As with most trimarans, *Swingaway*'s floats provided a convenient way on board when she was beached, and an even easier one for bathers and mermaids when she was in the water. Her floats, shaped like miniature submarines, rode low, often completely submerged when there was anything of a sea. Ken had told me where the key was stowed, inside the binnacle hanging on a pipe that led to the engine, and after groping round at arm's length I found it and opened the cabin door.

The interior of the boat and especially the forward cabin was crammed with gear – piles of blue-covered foam cushions from the cockpit, a rubber dinghy, oars, life-belts, a boat-hook. But behind the disorder it all looked comfortable, well arranged and good. Everything was well finished and of the best materials, and the layout was an orderly miracle of compactness – a mass of equipment fitted like a Chinese puzzle into a handful of space. In the centre of the main cabin, to starboard of the gangway to the fo'c'sle, was a formica table with cushioned seating round – lowered it made a double bed. Underneath it was the centre-board casing and an ice-box/refrigerator. At the after end of the main cabin to starboard was the galley with sink (salt and fresh water), shelves, cupboards and gas-cooker (grill, oven and two burners). Opposite to port was a navigation table, chart stowage, bookshelf, echo-sounder and gas-leak detector. Much of the navigation table was occupied by a radio-telephone but this was something Ken would transfer to his new boat. On the rest of the port side a cushioned seat ran forward, cut short of full sleeping length to accommodate a red paraffin heater with a chimney to the deck.

Forward of the main cabin were the heads (I could hardly get the door open for gear) with a wash-basin that pulled forward over the WC. This little compartment would shut up and serve as a shower-room, the water running away to the bilge. Forward again were two single bunks with a port-hole each and a generous shelf running along the hull beside each one. The bunks were staggered to allow for a hanging wardrobe at the head of the starboard one.

In the cockpit, mounted on the bulkhead of the main cabin were a series of gauges and indicators: to starboard a speed-and-distance log, a wind-speed indicator and a ships-head-and-wind indicator; to port another speed indicator, its dial reading from a Walker log trailed astern, and a bracket and connection for an echo-sounder then dismounted for safe stowage. There were heavy teak gratings, seats all round, canvas dodgers and in the centre of the cockpit a binnacle which carried a light and a compass in gimbals. In the cockpit there was access to the two 25-gallon watertanks, and to the four-cylinder Watermota petrol engine. At the stern there was a wind-vane fitted for self-steering with direct lines to the tiller, and there was a hand bilge-pump under one of the seats. There was in addition an electric bilge-pump operated by a switch in the cabin.

It was all very impressive and it needed only one thing to settle it. The mast had been unstepped from its pulpit on the deck and was nowhere to be seen. I went off to enquire after it and was told it was on the quay near the travelling hoist. This was next to the marina proper where most of the yachts were lying moored to floating wooden stages with water and electricity laid on. I took the opportunity to wander round, look at some of the boats, and walk to the end of one of the jetties and the entrance to the river where the tide was running out down to the Solent. Then I walked back to the hoist which was in use, its broad slings being put under a yacht in the water prior to hoisting it out. There were several masts lying on the quay, but one of the yard people picked out *Swingaway*'s mast for me. There it was with the stays and shrouds still attached to it. As for the stainless steel rigging, it shone as brightly as the knives on a dinner table, and the main stays and shrouds were as thick as my thumb. There was strength and to spare. I drove back to town in an excited mood and rang Ken the next day. I seemed to have found a boat.

The next thing was to settle about the price and the equipment. Not long after, Ken managed to call in at my place in Clapham on a rushed visit to London. We had morning coffee together and we went over two lists of equipment Ken brought with him — what he proposed to leave on the boat and what he wanted to take off. The former made a pretty complete inventory, and the latter included mainly things I didn't want or already had. After some good-natured horse trading Ken accepted an offer of £6000 subject to survey. It is true I had already got this for *Pussy Cat*, but there was agent's commission to be deducted in that case, and I anticipated I would have to spend possibly up to £1000 on fitting out.

The first item Ken wanted to take was the radio telephone. With a range of 50 miles or so, this is not much use if you are 1000 miles from the nearest land and possibly 500 from the nearest ship. On a coastal cruise it may be handy to get a Post Office link and ring up the office, but for some people the essence of sailing is to get away from it all — no telephone, no television, no news. The dinghy also was not included, but I already had one with a tiny seagull outboard. I had changed over to a rubber dinghy after a series of mishaps when trying to tow plastic and wooden dinghies in rough seas. Twice they broke away and were lost, and in any case they take a good deal of way off a small yacht. Rubber dinghies go round in circles instead of in a straight line, and in rough harbours the smaller ones are inclined to become paddling pools rather than boats, wetting both passengers and baggage. They are hard to row in high winds and chasing a runaway dinghy in a big harbour can be as frustrating as chasing a hat on a windy day. But for all that, their advantages outweigh their drawbacks. One can simply let the air out, fold them up and stow them under a bunk on a long passage. And the better ones are very tough. I had one ten years old and with a few patches, still going as strong as ever.

Again Ken wanted to keep his life-raft. I had never had one on *Pussy Cat*, all our voyages having been within reach of the coast or in busy shipping lanes. The case of multihulls is rather different from monohulls for the boat itself can be made into a life-raft of a kind. If holed or swamped by heavy seas a monohull will go straight to the bottom, as many tragic accidents show. A life-raft is as much part of her safety equipment as life-buoys, life-jackets or safety-harness. Multihulls can sink in the same way (there is the case of Nigel Tetley's *Victress* in point) for if the hull has no built-in buoyancy, the weight of the equipment will sink it. But without the enormous weight of a keel, it is possible to seal off parts of the hull or include air-chambers of one kind or another (for instance much air is trapped in a foam sandwich construction) with enough positive buoyancy to keep the hull afloat if swamped or holed, or even if broken apart. There have been several cases of multihulls damaged in a collision, say, and abandoned by their crew, then drifting round the Channel for days or weeks to be later salvaged or washed ashore and gradually broken up. But in winter conditions or if far out to sea, it may not be possible to survive for long in a swamped hull, or worse perhaps, one that has capsized. As important as the inflation which keeps the life-raft afloat, is the hood which keeps out wind and spray. This was something I would have to get.

The only other large item Ken would be keeping was the self-steering gear. In addition to the simple wind-vane with direct lines to the tiller which was fitted as standard equipment, Ken had a 'Tiller Mate', a sophisticated piece of apparatus with an electric motor driven from the batteries, which would steer either from a special electric compass keeping the boat on a predetermined compass course, or from a wind-vane keeping the boat on a course related to the wind and varying with it. I had already thought of buying one of these and Ken's experience helped me decide to do so. He had found it excellent in use, especially when steering by compass, though he had found the tiny wind-vane too volatile in normal conditions, and had not been able to damp it down satisfactorily.

Apart from these items, the boat was very well equipped indeed. The deal was as good as settled, and it was only a matter of arranging a survey. I first asked a high-powered firm in Chichester, but they were going to send two men over to Lymington and charge in the region of £150 so I politely ducked. Then I made some local enquiries and got a well-qualified man in Lymington at less than a third of the fee. He looked at the boat the same week and gave me a very full report which was 99 per cent favourable. The boat he found sound and strongly built and was particularly impressed by the rigging. His 1 per cent reservation was the bearing of the propeller shaft, which he reported to be worn and recommended it be replaced. When I got in touch with Ken he agreed to pay for the work, and asked me to get it done through the yard. This slight defect was something the surveyor mentioned in good faith – indeed he was bound to do so. However, as it happened, it was to lead to a train of accidents. Of which more in due course.

3
Best Buy

THE arrangement for sharing with Ken was a success so far as I was concerned, and I think for him too. He told me well in advance that he would like to have the boat for a week or so in May, for a few week-ends, and for a longer cruise (up to four weeks) in July when he intended to go west from Saint Malo along the coast of Brittany. He also proposed to sail in the Round-the-Island Race at the beginning of July. This suited me, as all I wanted to do, all I had time to do, was to get to know the boat as well as possible and get her fitted out, again as well as possible. I planned to get away at the end of the summer and the month of August would do as well as any.

Ken generously offered to take me out for a week-end and show me how everything worked, and also invited me to come along on the Round-the-Island Race. He ran a manufacturing business in Nottingham which had been his father's and he was extremely practical. The firm made knitting-machines which sold all over the world, and perhaps because of his association with the factory, he could turn his hand to installation or repair of anything connected with the yacht. He enjoyed demonstrating how all the bits and pieces worked or fitted together, and since it was all of prime importance to me, he couldn't have had a more attentive or interested audience. Not that I was as adept or knowledgeable where anything mechanical (particularly the engine and the electrics) was concerned. Ken once described himself to me as a gadget man, but he was more than that, for on the sailing side he handled *Swingaway* with easy confidence. He had an equally efficient partner in his wife Ann. I have known a number of sailing ladies who have all had their good qualities, but for pleasant cruising Ann was a paragon. She was a competent helmswoman and knowledgeable about pilotage and coastal navigation. The boat, and especially the galley, was spotless, and on the short cruise I went on, she managed the catering with unobtrusive ease and appetising results.

We all met first for a picnic one week-end when *Swingaway* was still ashore. This time I did the honours, producing smoked chicken and a bottle of champagne. Ken had offered to paint the bottom of the boat with anti-fouling and he and Ann were just finishing the job when I arrived. Like the day I first saw the boat it was lovely weather and we sat in the cockpit in the sun with our respective cars parked beside the boat on the gravel and a view of cows and fields and hedgerows beyond. When we opened the champagne I went up forward and poured a little over the bow as a libation. For a liner that is going to carry thousands of passengers and millions of tons of cargo, it may require a whole bottle to propitiate the gods of the sea, but I thought that for *Swingaway* a glass would be sufficient sacrifice. Perhaps if I had been more generous, our troubles at sea might have been fewer.

Having finished the anti-fouling Ken spent much of the afternoon going over all the gear. There were two good-capacity batteries and the wiring was planned to protect the one that started the engine from being drained by the lights. All the electrics and the fuse-board were easily accessible just inside the main cabin and they kept dry even during the roughest passages. But as for the circuit and its protective 'blocking diode' I never really understood it, and despite all our care both batteries did eventually go flat. Another rather baffling instrument was the ship's-head-and-wind-direction gauge which had a tiny losenge-shaped ship on the dial and an arrow to represent the wind. The trouble was that the little ship would stick in one position and refuse to move round the dial. Ken could always coax it into life by dismantling the back, but it was beyond me. It enabled the helmsman to keep on a fixed course in relation to the wind simply by watching the dial. Not much use during the day, when I prefer to gauge the look of the sails, the feel of the wind and the heel of the boat and its way through the water. But it would have been useful at night when all these factors are more difficult to judge. The electric log beside it functioned throughout, even generating its own night-light, and so did the wind gauge until the fitting was wrenched off the mast in a gale. Though not instrument-minded I found the mast-head wind-gauge very good, much better than looking round and estimating 'about Force 5' (on the principle that what was good enough for Beaufort was good enough for me) or using a hand-gauge at deck level and adding a percentage to get the wind speed aloft.

One gadget that never registered anything but *Safe* was the Sniffette, an artificial nose with its sense of smell in the bilge and a dial marked *Safe, Gas, Danger, Explosive*. Though we had quite a lot of petrol and five containers of gas on board we never had any leaks. There seems to be no straightforward answer to the question of safe fuels. I only once had a fire on board a boat and that was caused by a paraffin cooker. Somehow the paraffin flooded out and went on fire. Like a lunatic, instead of using one of the three fire extinguishers, I seized the flaming stove, hurled it into the cockpit and threw a bucket of water over it, which by the grace of God put it out. I lost my front hair and eyebrows and my face swelled up like a balloon, but I recovered in a few days. I did meet one man who had his £8000 dream boat actually blown up. It was going to take him and his family from England to New Zealand and having a phobia about fire or explosion on board he decided petrol, gas and paraffin were all too dangerous. So he got a very expensive stove using diesel oil. He was cruising down the Channel when there was a thunderous explosion, he was thrown into the water and the boat sank. On top of everything the diesel stove had cost so much he hadn't been able to insure the boat. 'I don't really know what happened,' he told me, 'but I'm sure it was the diesel cooker. Something got blocked, the pressure built up, and wham!'

Then there was the engine. The Watermota was a standard Ford engine in nautical disguise. As a petrol engine it was far quieter and with less vibration than a diesel and didn't weigh so much. They were supposed to be less reliable at sea, but this one gave no trouble so long as it was treated right. The only persistent fault was a loose belt to drive the alternator which seemed to recur whatever we did to fix it. The engine did play up on its first trial after the winter and even Ken was baffled, but in the end it proved to be due to a sparkplug with an intermittent fault.

More in my unmechanical line was a bright red paraffin heater. Unfortunately the spray-proof cowl on top of the chimney, which let in water in rough weather, was set so near the deck it was impossible to fix a plastic cover over it. It took up so much room that what should have been a fifth bunk was cut down to a 4-foot seat. A third drawback was that most of the heat went up the chimney. On all counts a portable oil stove firmly fixed in place would have been better. On the other hand the water-tanks were ideal. They held a good 50 gallons and were built with an interconnecting pipe so that, though it was quicker to fill them separately, water could be pumped until both were empty. Because of the separation there was no rolling in a sea as there might have been with one big tank. They had strong, well-designed lids which never leaked or came loose but were easy to open and close. Most important, the lids were large enough to allow a whole arm into the tanks for cleaning. Low enough for stability and ease of access, they were just under the floor of the cockpit.

The Calor-gas cylinder in use was under a seat in the forward starboard corner of the cockpit. The surveyor remarked on the fact that the tube to the stove was copper and suggested a flexible connection would be safer. I changed it for heavy duty rubber, but I think I might have saved myself that trouble. The copper was not all that rigid, could bend easily and I doubt if it would have fractured. The hand bilge-pump on the port side of the cockpit was a Whale under part of the seat which lifted. With a good-sized-diameter pipe, it never gave any trouble and only once needed cleaning out and the rubber gaskets or washers reseating or replacing. The second bilge-pump we hardly used, firstly to save the batteries since it was electric, and secondly because as it was fitted it didn't pump the bilges as dry as the hand pump. The intake was a narrow-bore pipe whose metal filter had corroded, and I had difficulty finding non-corrosive metal gauze to replace it. In the end I made do with a perforated zinc sheet, not as good as a wire mesh. The echo-sounder had a permanent bracket in the cabin where it was safe from spray or (in port) light fingers. A tiny hole in the bulkhead for its rubber connection and another bracket in the cockpit made it possible to take continuous soundings from the helm when in shallow water or coming into port.

The compass in gimbals in a white plastic binnacle in the centre of the cockpit was well situated in relation to the tiller and had a good shaded light for night sailing. Ken used little fairy lights from Christmas trees. They had bulbs no bigger than a grain of rice with two wires like spider's web sprouting from the bulb. I had only seen the bigger Christmas tree lights joined in a festoon, but I searched for and found a supply of these lilliput bulbs, and they proved satisfactory until, after days of drenching seas and pouring rain, various lash-ups (which also failed in time) became necessary. The compass itself was a Sestrel with a grid made by Henry Browne of Leadenhall Street. The grid fitted over the compass and had two heavy black parallel lines which could be set so that on whatever course you happened to be, the North-and-South line of the compass would be between the two black lines. Thus instead of having to peer at degrees on a dial (the old compass rose, like a spiky flower with 32 petals, is easier to see than our modern dials) it was only necessary to keep the North-South lubber-line within the grid lines to know one was on the right course. This is a device for those who like it. I found it useful over long, not-too-concentrated periods. With frequent or sudden alterations at short notice, I had to work out the relation between the compass, the grid, the tiller and the boat from scratch, and easily got muddled. But then I don't react instantly to right-left directions and follow Chinese street directions more quickly – 'First east, second north, first west, then on the south-hand side.' In its binnacle, the compass was fitted in a depression which made it difficult to take visual bearings, though it protected it from knocks. However by the time we set out we had two hand-bearing compasses: a Sailor with a Beta light for night use, and a Seafix with a tiny bulb that would light a magnifying prism.

The design of the cockpit on two levels worked well. The after part of the tiller and binnacle was higher and this gave good visibility over the cabin top and all round. The forward part being lower was more sheltered in bad weather, and though there were all-round canvas dodgers, we rarely used them, preferring to crouch behind the cabin top just peering over the edge. It also meant there were fewer steps down to the cabin. The cockpit was big enough for a party and there were all-round cushions, foam rubber and PVC covers with zips. These we left behind when we finally set sail. There was the danger of losing them overboard, the zips would get thoroughly corroded and it would very likely be the end of the covers themselves.

I've mentioned a lot of gear connected with navigation. This equipment is to the navigator what her *batterie de cuisine* is to the housewife. Some things are essential, others marginal, others a matter of personal taste or the depth of one's pocket. A cooking stove (or a compass) is essential. But while one person may swear by an electric liquidiser (or a radar set), another may make as appetising a meal (or as safe a passage) with a simple grater (or a hand radio-direction finder). In neither case does an elaborate array of equipment ensure results. Again what applies to top-class international racing may not apply to cruising. Racing cars are very different from the average run-about. Or to continue the kitchen simile, boiling an egg for breakfast is a different matter from cooking a five-course Christmas dinner for a dozen people.

This brings me to the galley. On a trimaran the problem of heeling is not so serious as on a monohull. Things jump about on occasion, but no gimbals are necessary and if you don't fill containers too full or leave cups and plates on the edge of the table, they mostly stay put. Also *Swingaway*'s galley was particularly well designed. The stove being against the after bulkhead just by the door to the cockpit, there was less likelihood of getting fumes in the cabin, and it was handy both to the cockpit and to the table which was within reach just forward. The space between the stove and a 4-ft-high divide which formed the back of the table seating, was large enough to work in, but small enough for the cook to wedge himself in place with everything manoeuvrable, everything to hand, and yet keeping steady even in rough weather. I have seen a galley on a £50,000 yacht four times the size and equipped like the Ritz, that was not only more inconvenient, but positively dangerous in a heavy sea.

When the cook was facing the stove with a view aft through the door to the cockpit, he had on his left the sink and draining-board-work-table, and only had to turn to get crockery, cutlery, open a tin, chop up a salad or wash the dishes. There was a wall tin-opener, roll of tissues (even more useful at sea than in the kitchen) and the sink had salt and fresh water. Behind and below the sink was stowage and above it a port-hole. With more stowage opposite the stove under the seat, there was room to store everything regularly needed. Unlike some boats, there was generally little need to move A, B and C to get at D, a process which can become wearisome if stowage is too short or badly arranged.

While the boat was on shore it was easy to work on the bottom and the floats, and I went round greasing the bolts of the girders where they joined the joints of the outriggers and where they joined the main hull. I also went round the floats at the waterline where a plastic-and-rubber rubbing-strake was fixed on, and made as sure as I could that it was watertight. One likes to be able to see everything or be sure if not that there is no hidden corrosion, decay or water getting in. The floats were permanently sealed and filled with foam. Ken said that after several seasons he had holes bored in the bottom and only about a gallon of water drained out of each float. However an Ocean Bird owner I met in Las Palmas had a different experience, of which more anon.

I painted the cockpit. The original fibreglass finish after half-a-dozen seasons was beginning to lose its shine and become crazed and marked here and there. I gave it two coats of white, two-can polyurethane and it looked like new. The stainless steel railings of the taffrail had been taken off to straighten a bend caused by an argument with a jetty, and these were put back by the yard in the next weeks. It took longer to get the work done which the surveyor had recommended and they were working on the prop shaft and the bearing at the stern the day before the boat was due to go into the water.

The launching was on a Wednesday in April. I went down to Lymington on Tuesday and watched the man from the yard working on the stern bearing. The yard (Websters) was at the entrance to the marina, busy with boat-building, repairs and chandlery. The marina office was near the quays and looked after the boats in the water, ran the travelling hoist, and would also put owners in touch with independent mechanics, riggers, carpenters etc. for small jobs. There was enough work all round to keep everybody happy.

I started painting the topsides of the floats with two coats of the same as the cockpit. I slept the night on board, *Swingaway*'s last night ashore. It was cold with stars in a clear sky and I was glad to light the paraffin heater. I couldn't use the sink or WC on board, so fed on sandwiches and used the Portaloo in the marina to which all boat-owners had a key. In the morning I finished painting the floats and went for a walk through the marshes south of the marina. There was dew on the grass and the breath of the cows turned to steam in the cold air. Over the low land I could see the masts of a boat in the Solent moving west, approaching Hurst Castle and the narrowest part of the Needles Channel.

About eleven two men came and put slings under the boat, but it was not until lunch-time that the mobile box-crane came slowly up on its huge rubber tyres and straddled the yacht. Slowly they hauled her off the wooden blocks and the crane rolled down towards the launching dock, *Swingaway* rocking lightly in the slings. Soon she was in the water and a workboat standing by had her in tow, taking her round to Berth K 24. This was Ken's permanent berth, paid for by the year, but if he was away cruising the marina could let it temporarily to a visiting yacht. I went on board again, washed her down and filled the water tanks. She looked good lying there alongside the teak jetty. I pottered round inside, opening stop cocks, trying out the toilet and the water to the sink. Everything worked. Now she was in the water I would have liked to stay on board, but I had to go for I had other things to do. But I didn't get back to London until late that night. So much for the boat. Just as important, or more so, was the crew.

4
'Men are not measured by Inches'

So says an old proverb. No doubt it refers to intellectual and spiritual qualities. But even in physical terms height doesn't give the same advantage in sailing that it does in tennis or in the rugby line-out. For some jobs on board it's useful to be big and strong and able to reach another six inches up the mast. But the cramped quarters of many small sailing boats don't suit six-footers, and a sense of balance, surefootedness and the ability to cling like a leech when the boat lurches or is swept by a wave, are qualities just as likely to be found in those of stocky build. Even in these days of safety harness, 'always have a hand for the ship' is as good advice as it was for those who went to sea in wind-jammers. In the end, though, it's temperament that counts, certainly on a long cruise.

For numbers I wanted enough but not too many. Every extra hand eases the work of night watches, cleaning, maintenance and handling. The more crew the more berths, the more food and water, the more baggage, the more weight, the less room. One has to pick the boat for the crew and the crew for the boat, and then again the boat for the money. Pull here, push there, and finally it seems to fit together – more or less. If, like the racing headliners, you have a sponsor with hundreds or thousands to spend, it's a different matter. For *Swingaway* I thought three would be about right. A roomy cockpit, a comfortable main cabin, a smallish fo'c'sle. There were two singles and a double berth, but the double was troublesome. It meant lowering the table and fitting an extra foam cushion across it. Night after night over a long period this would become quite a chore. Anyway who was going to share a double bunk for three months at sea? Snoring was one thing but coping with the rolling of even the lightest bedfellow for a hundred-and-one nights was another. Would I take women? They were fine on a short or medium cruise, but on a long one? Most likely it would be three men, or if a woman she would have to come on practical merit and strictly in her own bunk.

How about my nearest and dearest? Some sailing enthusiasts go out on short or long cruises as a family. I had had family sailing holidays (with mixed success) and all the family had come out with me individually. But none of them had taken it up for themselves. Like all sensible women, my wife regarded sailing as a quite unnecessary combination of discomfort, danger and futility. In any case all the children were grown up and had their jobs or marriages, or both, to prevent them from coming with me.

I advertised through the Cruising Association, yachting journals and an agency that ran a Cruise Index for owners and crews. 'Crew for ocean voyage small yacht. South Africa, Australia, New Zealand.' In my last boat I had taken in total maybe up to 40 people, and had found that these media were the best for getting crew. Readers of the national dailies and weeklies are mostly looking for easy (some would say empty) cellophane-wrapped diversion or glamour – not escape to discomfort and adventure. Several of the people who had come with me on previous voyages would have been ideal. There was Pete, that practical genius who had rigged up a water-cooling system for an outboard engine in ten minutes. There was Danny the lorry-driver, as solid as one of his own lorries but more reliable, there was Rosalie who played the guitar, Jenny who steered us up the Thames at night, Roger who enjoyed a good storm, Peter who knew the Channel Islands like his back garden. Alas, I wasn't in a position to persuade any of them to give up their jobs even for a short time. I did ask Brian, once in the merchant marine, as he was a self-employed film-effects man, but having had a long break the previous year, he couldn't afford to go away again so soon.

There were plenty of applications from the advertisements. There was David, an Australian journalist who sounded very knowledgeable on the phone and was thoroughly nice when I met him though he hadn't done much sailing. There was Richard, a school-teacher who wanted to come only as far as the Canaries. There was Peter who was very keen but aged only nineteen. There was Jeff, a draughtsman in the City. There was Rupert, a public-school boy sailing since he was seven and now aged eighteen. There was another Peter, a tool-maker, with a provincial accent that made him sound both practical and reliable, and who could turn his hand to 'most kinds of engines'. Here was someone who would make up for my mechanical shortcomings. Even more so David, a Kiwi tool-maker, who was qualified (mark you) in 'marine electronics' which I supposed meant batteries, lights, circuits, direction-finders and radio sets. What a boon on a long voyage. Somehow he faded out. There was James from South Shields, another down-to-earth candidate; Mr Morgan from the Isle of Man who had been a steward and stoker in the merchant service; Mr Dean from Stockport who had done some dinghy sailing; Mr Field from Birmingham who was in the taxi business. There was Malcolm from Durham, a sailing instructor with a mechanic's certificate, there was Dave aged twenty-one from Cowley, there was Paul aged twenty from Brussels, and Patrick also twenty from Westcliff.

I corresponded or spoke on the telephone to everybody. Some I thought too young, some clearly didn't have a clue about sailing or at any rate about a long cruise, some withdrew when I talked about the uncertainty of the voyage, the need to be able to look after themselves if we didn't make it (or if we did), the size of the boat, the cost of sharing provisions, fuel, charts, etc. There were two girls who got in touch. One wasn't serious, simply flirting with the idea – or ready to flirt with young yachtsmen. The other, a New Zealand girl who came from a sailing family, might have been excellent. She had sailed some 3000 miles as crew in the last two seasons, and sounded tough and pleasant. She had a friend who might be interested also and she would talk to him. But she rang up later to say she was going to be married and she couldn't manage it – not for the moment.

Over the weeks people seemed to sort themselves out, and in the end I had three possibles. There was Peter (a third Peter), Bob and Jack. Jack had written from Middlesbrough. He had been twelve years in the Navy and about a year ashore, working as a stock controller for Tesco. His wife hadn't had much sailing experience but she could cook and wanted to come. After talking over the phone it was arranged that we would meet in London on Saturday morning and drive down to the boat and I would drop them somewhere on Sunday to get a train back to Middlesbrough. I met Jack outside the hotel near Earls Court where they had spent the night, looking (as he always did) perfectly suited for the sea. He was dark, small, neatly built and his cap, jersey and anorak might just have come out of the shop. We got on easily from the start and I liked his wife Heather, not a glamour-puss but attractive and quiet. Jack and I did most of the talking as we drove down – about the boat, about the week-end, about his family (in the West Country), about their work up north and plans to emigrate.

It was the third time I had been out in the boat and we had a pleasant sail in the Solent, coming back to the marina for the night. Again on Sunday we went out in the morning and then later that evening I dropped them at Euston. We parted saying we would both think about it, but I had pretty well decided I would have to turn them down. It seemed to me that Heather had hardly ever been in a boat before and I didn't think she was very happy. Jack had been good company, seemed at home on the boat and his expert knowledge as a trained signaller might come in useful. I wondered if I could get four on board but decided it would be too crowded for so long. There was no help for it. I wrote to say I would have been glad to take Jack as one of the crew, but I didn't think Heather had had enough sailing experience and I thought the voyage would be too tough for her.

I might not have had the courage to put Heather and Jack off, if I hadn't met Bob just the previous day. He was a Kiwi, a rugger player, big and strong and good humoured. He had taken a maths degree, done some teaching and was seeing a bit of the world, intending eventually to make his way back to New Zealand. He had digs in Ealing and was working on a building site with Irish labourers, but there was nothing very permanent about it. I wanted Bob to come down and see the boat, but Ken and Ann were going out the next week-end so it was two weeks before I picked him up to drive down on Friday. I had asked two others to join us – two of the three Peters. One was the tool-maker and mechanic, Peter Kilduff, and the other, Peter Cole, had telephoned just that week from Colchester, sounded cheerful and confident and said he was a diver, had spent some years in Australia and the South Seas, and wanted to go back. They were both to join us in the marina on Saturday. Bob and I got down early Friday evening and made ourselves comfortable. It was too late to go out, but we got the floats out ready for the next day. Although the marina berths were only wide enough for a single hull, the other half of *Swingaway*'s bay was still vacant as there were no visiting yachts. Though we had to fold in the wings whenever we left the boat, it was possible to lie with them out for a night without moving to an outside berth.

The business of getting the floats out or folding them in had to be planned to fit in with leaving and entering port according to circumstances. If *Swingaway* was under sail, the floats had to be out (except perhaps going into harbour under jib alone with a light following wind) but she could motor in reasonably sheltered waters or good weather, with the floats folded in and lashed to the hull. They folded back towards the stern, so if the boat was under way this kept them against the hull. It also made it more difficult to get them out if the boat was going forward, and in those early weekends when the joints were stiff after a winter's disuse, this was a factor to take into account. The girders of galvanised iron tube were held by fibreglass collars which were held tight by sets of bolts. Altogether there were thirty-two bolts to loosen or tighten, but with a ratchet spanner it was quick work. The first time it took me almost two hours using tackle, blocks and finally the sheet winches to move the floats, but with plenty of grease they eased more and more until they could be moved by hand except for the first few inches. Even so it was easier to get them out at leisure alongside, rather than under way. Once out they were rigidly held by two cross stays of heavy stainless-steel wire, and they never gave any trouble in weeks at sea. But I had some anxious moments going into crowded harbours with a flood tide, wondering if they would fold in in time.

The next day we waited for the two Peters while, after breakfast, I showed Bob over the boat and we pottered about doing minor chores and discussing gear and arrangements that might be useful on a long voyage. I remember we exercised our brains on how to fit a temporary fiddle round the formica-top table. We tried glueing a metal and then a plastic strip round the edge, but they wouldn't stick firmly and in any case weren't high enough to stop a runaway saucer. In the end we put a couple of cheap rubber mats on the table which worked well. We had some spillage and breakages, but only one through things falling off the table. Peter from Colchester turned up about 11 a.m. and in the afternoon we got under way, motoring down the river to the Solent for another day sail. Over lunch and that evening when we got back, Peter told us about his adventures in the South Seas. He had been working on a partnership basis with a group of Australians in a boat the size of a fishing trawler in Pacific Islands where there were war wrecks, collecting scrap metal. They worked under water with skin-diving gear and oxy-acetylene equipment, cutting away copper, bronze and the like until they had a boat-load to take back to Sydney. It was killing work but profitable business and they were making good money. It was dangerous too. Not only did they have to be careful about the depths and the time they stayed under, they also had encounters with sharks. One man had been attacked. Peter had a nasty accident on the boat and in a rough sea had fallen and hurt his eye on a projecting part of an air-compressor standing on deck. They got him to Sydney and into hospital as soon as possible but it was too late to save his eye and he was fitted out with a glass one. I thought there was something odd about his sight but hadn't realised he was blind in one eye until he told us. It wasn't easy to tell by looking at him because the eye was a perfect match, but it was the way he moved and turned his head and did things, making one eye do the work of two.

The loss of his eye hadn't stopped him diving but then their boat sank. It was by no means a new boat and after a spell of bad weather it had sprung a leak when on passage between the islands. Though they pumped their guts out, the water kept gaining and it was clear they weren't going to make it. So they launched the ship's boat and watched their trawler follow the war-time wrecks into the depths. They were some 50 miles from the nearest island, the weather wasn't too bad by then, and they managed to get to land after a couple of nights at sea. This put an end to their venture and Peter decided to come home at least for a holiday and to see his family. Now after four months he was getting bored and wanted to get back to the Pacific for some more action. That was his story and he produced a cutting half-a-mile long from the local paper to confirm it.

We had an enjoyable week-end and all got on well together. Though we waited a bit, the second Peter, the tool-maker, didn't turn up. I was in half a mind to settle for Bob and Peter the diver as crew, though I had some doubts whether Peter might not get restless and bored on a slow passage. Also I wondered about his eye. Moving about a small boat at sea, handling sails and fixing gear, one needs to be sharp and alert. I had to be away for a week at a film festival in France, and it was agreed we would all think about it and be in touch in ten days time. Then when I got back from the festival, there was a letter from Jack. He and Heather had talked things over and he would like to come on his own. She would stay in England and join him later. There seemed no doubt that Jack was better qualified than Peter for a long sailing voyage. Bob I was settled about. I asked Bob if he had any strong views, but he said he would be easy whether Peter came or somebody else. The thing to do it seemed, was to have another week-end on the boat, Jack, Bob and me and see how we got on. And soon. The end of June was upon us and if we were to get away before the autumn, it ought to be settled. One thing I was sure about as a result of our short trips: it would be a mistake to have more than three on board.

Both Jack and Bob could manage the next week-end. Jack came

by train on Friday night, stayed overnight with me, and we picked up Bob before eight o'clock in the morning. We made a good start from the marina by lunch and sailed east through the Solent against the tide but with a good following breeze to Wootton Creek for the night. We tried out the spinnaker for the first time and we were getting more used to the boat. We motored up towards Ryde and found a good anchorage away from moorings. Bob turned out some well-grilled chops and we had a quiet night. We made an early start to catch the tide and tacked our way down the Solent to arrive back at Lymington by 1030, having passed several yachts on the way.

This seemed to be it. Together as a crew we hoped to reach New Zealand and as we saw it then, the voyage fell into four parts. First there was the comparatively easy run down to the Canaries. Then came the passage from the Canaries to Cape Town, the longest and hardest stretch, for it meant fighting our way south against the Trades and before that coping with the calms of the Doldrums. Across the Indian Ocean in the summer the Forties might not roar quite so loudly and at least we could count almost 90 per cent on following winds. In the last stage we would go from Perth to Melbourne and then either straight across to Auckland or up to Sydney before we tackled the Tasman. But that was a long way ahead. Built into all our discussions was the possibility that we might have to give up at any stage – or for that matter between stages.

We discussed gear, provisions, what have you. We would set out by the end of August which would give us the spring and summer months in the Southern Hemisphere. If we had to pack up at any stage Bob and Jack would be able to look after themselves. Wherever we got to, they would be able to live on board in port for at least a month. I would supply the boat equipped for off-shore cruising and the others would pay me £70 each towards the boat and any repairs. We would share the cost of provisions, fuel, charts, and they would have a say in whatever was bought. Everybody would do a bit of everything and we would share sailing the boat, watches, cooking, chores. However, I would have special responsibility for navigation, Jack for signals, radio and RDF (radio direction finding), Bob for the engine and lights. We would take the boat down to Teignmouth for the builders to have a look at her and set sail from there. One difficult job remained. I wrote to Peter the diver in Colchester and said I was sorry.

5
Fitting Out

I HAD now been out in *Swingaway* half-a-dozen times, and had got the feel of her, and liked her. The first and last occasions were with Ann and Ken. The first was at the beginning of their Easter holiday before they went along the coast when we went across for a night to Newtown River, the second was the Round-the-Island Race at the beginning of their cruise to France. In between, besides getting crew, I had been busy enough with various items of equipment.

For the cruise to Newtown River we had perfect weather and the sun shone on the empty green fields that surround one of the most secluded havens in the Solent. Unlike some multihulls that rove like restless dogs in the night when at anchor, *Swingaway* lay as peaceful as a baby and I slept like one too. We had the place to ourselves and in the morning, encouraged by the sunshine, I lowered myself into the chilly water before breakfast, and swam round the boat. The water was cold but clean, unlike most of the Solent harbours, including Lymington, where it was only possible to bathe in an open-air swimming pool next to the marina. I came out with an edge like a razor to my appetite to find Ann supervising breakfast – fresh coffee, and toast with sausages and bacon gently sizzling under the grill. During the week-end Ken was able to continue the explanations he had started on shore and show me most of the gear under working conditions.

Though *Swingaway* came so well equipped, there were a number of things to think about for a long voyage. I have always found electricity a problem. Sooner or later one always seems to take more out of the batteries than one puts in. On *Pussy Cat* I had had a tiny generator called a Champ but its charge rate was far too low. I didn't want to buy a bigger generator both because of expense and weight. A Tilley lamp would help to save electricity in the evenings, we would run the engine regularly to charge the batteries, and as an auxiliary I bought a wind generator. It certainly helped us out but the rate of charge is rather low. They are most useful left on all week when the boat is at her mooring to provide electricity for the weekend. I also had to have a special fitting made which would bolt on to the stern railing, where the generator would get all the wind and be out of the way. After a lot of searching I found an engineering firm in London who agreed to make it in a chrome alloy for about £14.

Swingaway's sails were in quite good condition and very adequate. There was a mainsail, heavy genoa, working jib and storm jib by Bruce Banks, plus a light genoa and spinnaker by McKillop of Kingsbridge. The main had roller reefing, also reefing eyelets, and partial battens. The light genoa was cut rather low so that the foot hung over the stainless steel pulpit. This was a spot we had to watch for chafe, and the foot of the heavy genoa too lay along the guard wires and stanchions when it was sheeted in. The spinnaker was a jazzy black-and-orange affair, small enough to be used as a reaching sail in light winds. To this suit I proposed to add twin running sails. A quote from a firm at the Boat Show had worked out expensive so I went to see a local company, the Lymington Sail and Tent Company. Standing the right side of a large notice, DON'T WALK ON THE SAIL-CUTTING FLOOR, I waited until a tall stooping young man came over. I had taken the idea from the 'Fenger-Gill twins' described in the Amateur Yacht Research Association book on Self-Steering.

The sailmaker quickly gathered what I had in mind and asked knowledgeable questions about the beam, height of the mast, size of the fore-triangle etc. Then he showed me some samples of cloth. Most reasonable was a red nylon they used for spinnakers which he thought would be strong enough. It seemed I would be able to get the two sails for £70 to £80 and a second spinnaker pole would cost another £27. For the pole he had a do-it-yourself kit. You bought the aluminium tube, cut it to size, then riveted the fittings on. With a mast of 38 feet from the deck and poles of 13 feet, the sails were about 220 square feet each. This gave 400 square feet which before the wind should be enough for speeds of up to ten knots. The sailmaker sent a man down to put bolts in the deck just forward of the mast and about two feet apart. These would take the tack of the sail, the luff being inboard and actually aft of the leech since the poles would tilt forward from the mast. We would set them flying and use the spinnaker and jib halyards to hoist them. For self-steering we would take the sheets back on either side to the tiller. This self-steering worked without a hitch but we were to have trouble from chafing.

For sleeping we would use the bunk in the main cabin as a single and the two bunks in the fore-cabin. I would sleep in the main cabin where I would be on the spot and easy to call if anything happened. Bob and Jack would share the fore-cabin. Being near the bows of the ship there would be more movement and as there were no high bunk-boards, I reckoned to make the bunks more comfortable by fitting canvas sides which could be hooked up to the cabin top when it was rough, and tucked under the mattress during the day or in good weather. However Bob and Jack didn't seem to need them and they were never used. Either they were prehensile sleepers or the fore cabin wasn't as bad as I had thought. In the main cabin I used a piece of plywood to wedge myself in. One edge I stuck down beside the mattress, the other lay against the edge of the table. I got so dependent on the feeling of being held in, that I used it even in port.

For communications there was no reason to have a radio telephone. They are expensive, bulky and heavy on batteries. When we sailed *Pussy Cat* from Sweden we had a radio ham as one of the crew. In long sessions he only succeeded in making contact with four people ashore and then they were only able to wish each other well, send messages to the crew's girl friends and ask about the weather in Stockholm. At the same time by the fifth day he had run the batteries flat. However, in case of trouble, I bought a Safety Link, a one-way voice transmitter with a range of up to 50 miles and permanently tuned to the international distress frequency. Jack tried it once when we were near a French warship, but got no reply. It had a wider range than rockets or smoke signals though perhaps the latter are more certain. Of these we had a good supply: four parachute rockets; six red hand flares and three white; four small and one large orange smoke signals. Unfortunately when we were in trouble there were only albatrosses and porpoises to see them.

I already had a Sea-Fix for direction-finding. This had only one long-wave band, 200 to 400 Kc, which covers radio beacons everywhere and weather reports for shipping round the British Isles. In addition, in case the Sea-Fix went wrong and to extend the range of our reception for time signals, I got a Sailor Mariner Radio with a direction-finding attachment which cost nearly £300, and a Hitachi Navigator which was about £30. The Sailor had a fine hand-bearing compass but its RDF signal was no stronger than the Hitachi or the Sea-Fix. Both the Sailor and the Hitachi had more or less the same frequency coverage – the same long wave as the Sea-Fix, a medium band from 520 to 1600 Kc and a short-wave band from 1.6 to 12

Mgc. Unfortunately this did not cover some of the most useful continuous world time-signals. We had to depend on the BBC's eight or nine o'clock signal in the Overseas Service's short-wave broadcasts to Africa and South America. From this we did manage to get a signal most days, together with some news and occasional talks and records.

For timing sextant sights I thought of getting a chronometer, but for even a second-hand one I would have had to pay nearly £100. Also it would have been bulky, vulnerable in rough weather and hard to protect from damp. I had a self-winding Omega wrist-watch which had cost me £20 in 1958 and could still be relied on to within a minute a week. But its rate of loss seemed to alter, and though I tried to rate it before we left, I didn't get consistent results. We would have been in trouble, I think, without the daily time-signals.

For actually taking sights I had two Ebbco plastic sextants. They seemed quite satisfactory for sun sights and gave accurate enough results. However, for star sights they were more difficult to use, and the better eye-pieces of a more expensive instrument would have been a help. My navigation could hardly have been more rusty, since it went back to the war and the days of logarithms and cosines and long calculations. To brush up I first considered the formidable volumes of Nichol's *Concise Guide* and the Admiralty *Manual*, each as thick as a brick, and rapidly passed on to two smaller books, *Teach Yourself Navigation* (A.C. Gardner) and *Celestial Navigation for Yachtsmen* (Mary Blewitt). The first is excellent on chart work and dead reckoning and the second gives a thorough description of *the* easy method using tables (in my case *Sight Reduction Tables for Air Navigation*) to bypass all the trigonometry and logs. Nowadays I expect a GPS (Global Positioning System) the size of a large pocket calculator and costing about £1000 would save all this wet-towel book-work. It works off messages from satellites.

I got plenty of practice before we sailed by taking sights in my London flat. There is a good description of the method in *Teach Yourself Navigation*. An artificial horizon formed by a dish of water is substituted for the sea horizon, and you measure the angle between the sun and its reflection. It gives an angle double that of a normal sight so the reading simply has to be halved. I had tried this in the open air but found the water nearly always ruffled by the wind. Other liquids (I tried oil) didn't give a good reflection. But in the room (and the sun came streaming in from eleven to four) there was an untroubled reflection and peace and quiet, and the window pane didn't seem to cause any refraction. At least when I worked out the sights (looked up might be more appropriate for the method I used) the intercept ran clear through South London. I stuck to sun sights and to the same method until I knew it thoroughly. One or two nights I walked to Clapham Common to see if I could identify stars and sight them with the sextant. But the lights of London all around were so bright I could hardly see the sky, let alone any stars.

Finally I advertised for a second-hand life raft. The best offer seemed to be a four-man Beaufort about seven years old. The owners lived in a houseboat at Thames Ditton and were joining a group of six to sail an old-fashioned ketch to the West Indies. They had carried this life-raft on a smaller boat, but now with six in the crew needed a larger one. I went out to Thames Ditton and after negotiating some perilous gang-planks through a maze of floating verandahs, had a look at it in its valise. It seemed all right except that the certificate was out of date. On the check list there were a number of items missing but they could all be easily replaced or carried separately – a knife, a whistle etc. There was also a patch on the valise, but I reckoned if it was good enough for the inspector it was good enough for me. So I agreed on the asking price of £70, subject to a current certificate. We carried the life-raft under a seat in the cockpit and beside it a 'survival pack' with iron rations wrapped in plastic. Lashed in front of the binnacle was a 5-gallon container of fresh water also ready to go overboard in an emergency.

My last sail with Ken and Ann on the Round-the-Island Race was early in July. I was keen to see how *Swingaway* would do on this 40-mile circular course against every imaginable size and type of yacht, and also to take part in one of the best known and biggest yacht races in the world. I had raced a day-boat in Hong Kong Harbour, and in *Pussy Cat* in the Crystal Trophy Race had slogged 300 miles down Channel, round the Wolf Rock and up to Plymouth, but this would be different. Ken was skipper and I would have no responsibility – except to enjoy a day out and the colourful sight of a great event in the sporting calendar.

Ken had asked two of his Nottingham friends, Eric and Mike, Osprey sailors with Midland accents rich as cheese, so there would be five of us on board. The race was to start from Cowes at dawn on Saturday – monohulls at times around 0515, multihulls half-an-hour later around 0545. We left Lymington on Friday after lunch for Cowes to spend the night there. As *Swingaway* could only sleep four I had got a bed for the night ashore. I woke myself at 0400, crept out of my tidy bed-and-breakfast house and through the sleeping town. Down by the quays there were boats everywhere and a fleet of launches ferrying crews. I soon got a lift to *Swingaway* at the mooring where I had left her the previous evening. Nobody on board was ready to move when I arrived and Ann was first up. She started cooking breakfast and I defy anybody to sleep through the smell of bacon and eggs. Soon they were stumbling about, rehearsing sail changes, discussing the probable weather.

There was very little wind, just a gentle breeze from the northwest. It was misty and the visibility was only some 200 yards. As we lay at the mooring there were yachts all round us – yachts, yachts and more yachts. As time went they slipped their buoys, or cast off, or hoisted their anchors. More and more yachts came ghosting through the mist from further up the harbour and disappeared out towards the start. More and more and more . . . I had never seen so many. It was what I imagined Dunkirk was probably like – hundreds of small boats appearing in the haze of dawn.

Shortly after 0500 and in the wake of most of the fleet, we slipped the buoy and sailed out towards the long start line marked at its far end by a buoy well out into the Solent. We tacked out against the light northerly breeze and sailed up and down listening for the warning gun. The rest of the fleet was almost out of sight over the horizon towards Yarmouth as we crossed the line, a quarter of a minute behind the starting gun and slightly to the rear of our class of larger multihulls, the over-25-footers. Down past Yarmouth we could free the sheets a point or two and from Hurst Castle to the Needles it was half a reach. By now we were catching up and passing some of the smaller monohulls. Then round the Needles and running down to St Catherine's Point, the wind fresher and astern first on the starboard quarter, we got the spinnaker up and gradually worked our way into the middle of a sea of yachts of all shapes and sizes and colours, some with keen-looking racing crews, others with a happy-go-lucky, family picnic-party on board. The breeze held strong all day and gybing on to the port tack towards the south of the Island we still kept fairly well out, which seemed to pay, as we saw boats close inshore with sails almost empty. It was a glorious, blue-sky, come-to-the-fair day. There was 'racing-and-chasing-from-morning-to-night' for sure. But instead of roundabouts-turning there were yachts tacking, reaching, running, manoeuvring in all directions.

For lunch Eric and Mike handed out cans of beer while Ann passed round a variety of sandwiches, followed by coffee. On we sailed turning east and still passing much larger monohulls. Finally we had to lower the spinnaker and it was a beat up towards Bembridge and the forts at the entrance to the Solent. Now the monohulls were able to hold their own and it seemed that *Swingaway* was sailing at exactly the same speed as keelers foot-for-foot the same size. We would pass a yacht within a few feet heading on opposite tacks then after sailing half-an-hour or so, go about to pass them again in exactly the same relative position.

As the afternoon wore on we got up to the forts, but by then the tide had turned and was beginning to run east, while the wind had fallen. Some multihulls had long since finished and a second string of leaders, who were well into the Solent, added to their advantage because of the tide. By now we had developed a private race with another Ocean Bird, *Swing Wing*. Identical yachts, we somehow came together while passing the forts and going towards Ryde, and together tacked down the Solent. Finally right at the end, by persistently hugging the shore where the adverse tide was less, we gained the advantage and crossed the line a good five minutes ahead of the other boat. A minor triumph!

Swingaway finished a third way down the list of multihulls, which was not bad considering the weight of her equipment and the fact she had made no special preparation. The real speed came from three multihulls that led the combined fleet – *Three Cheers*, *Trifle*, and *Golden Cockerel*. *Three Cheers*, a remarkable trimaran designed in America by Richard Newick and sailed in the previous year's Singlehanded Transatlantic Race, broke the record for the course, covering the 65 miles in a unheard of 5½ hours – an average of nearly 12 knots in winds that were no more than moderate.

Eric and Mike were going to stay on board for the week-end and then Ken and Ann would take *Swingaway* for a two-week cruise. They planned to sail along the French coast between St Malo and Brest. But they were going back to Lymington first, so when we crossed the finishing-line, instead of going into Cowes, we carried on down the Solent using the engine to help stem the adverse tide. We made good time motor sailing and were alongside in the marina by 1800, ready for a sundowner.

6

DOWN THE CHANNEL

At the beginning of August, Bob, Jack and I planned to meet in Lymington, spend a few days there and then sail *Swingaway* down to Teignmouth, which is a few miles south of Exmouth. John Westell, the boat's designer, had agreed to vet *Swingaway* but warned me that the Teignmouth yard would be closing for a fortnight's summer holiday on the 20th. I wanted to have at least a week there in case there was some work to be done. Bob would give up his job at the end of July and come down to Lymington with me, and Jack would join us for the passage down Channel. He might have to spend some time in Middlesbrough before we sailed but it suited him to leave from Teignmouth as his parents lived nearby at Budleigh Salterton and he and Heather could stay with them while we were there.

Then about the time I was expecting a phone call from Ken, I had a letter. They had had a good cruise and visited several French ports, deciding however to come back a few days earlier than planned. They had used the engine from time to time and it seemed all right. Then on the last day as they were coming into the Solent, it began to vibrate suddenly, shook partially loose from its fixing (it was bolted to the frames through rubber shock-absorbers) and the exhaust-pipe had broken. They had managed to get in, and the engine itself seemed all right. He had found a nut in the bilge and he reckoned the workman who had renewed the stern bearing and prop shaft had failed to bolt the unit down firmly on both sides when he had finished the job. As they had come in at the week-end everything had been shut, but I could take it up with the boat-yard when I went down to Lymington. Though cross with the yard, he wrote in reassuring terms; but I imagined all sorts of trouble.

What a blow! A newly-acquired boat is like a new baby, and even a slight chill is as worrying as if grandma aged ninety-nine has a stroke. I could hardly wait to get down to the boat and see about it.

Bob and I drove down on Wednesday 1 August. The yard disclaimed responsibility and said they were sure the job had been properly done. I hadn't time to argue and as the yard couldn't do the repair immediately, I asked an independent mechanic who had tuned up the engine earlier in the season. He hummed-and-hawed about doing the job that week, but being an obliging young man finally agreed. When he took out the exhaust it was not only fractured but corroded and he proposed putting in a new one. He arrived the next day with a section of aluminium piping and heavy-duty rubber. 'This doesn't look so orthodox for an exhaust,' he said, 'but sea-water cooling means a cool exhaust. It'll give you a completely flexible coupling. You won't get another fracture from vibration.' He fitted the new exhaust, making a slight upward bend near the engine instead of (as with the old one) a big upward bend near the stern: an important difference in view of what occurred.

All this was done by the week-end, when he checked and tightened the bolting of the engine and propeller-shaft and presented what I reckoned a modest bill of £27. I wrote to Ken, sending the account, telling what the yard had said and leaving him to sort it out with them. I lost track of what ensued, but my impression was that indeed one of the bolts holding down the propeller shaft had not been properly secured. But who can prove these things? Often in this world the decision goes to whoever maintains his case most vehemently.

There were other jobs to think about. One of the frost-plugs in the engine was weeping. These springy dish-like metal caps are tapped into holes in the water-jacket so that if the engine freezes, the expanding ice will force them out and not crack the cylinder block. They are not likely to be necessary on a marine engine but were a vestige of the Watermota's land origin. After trying a number of garages I finally drove over to Hythe, 20 miles away. Besides the replacement I got two spares, but I should have got more.

Bob and I made up the new spinnaker-pole, spending a morning with a 'pop' riveter. When the wind was light enough we hoisted the twin-running sails to see if everything more or less fitted. One of the poles was a few inches longer than the other but it would not matter. Ken sent in the post a 'grab-it' boat-hook he had decided to leave on board and the Walker log taken by mistake with other gear. We fixed the WC, the first of many times, as the inlet valve was not closing tightly. We found a place to hang the Sea-Fix, where it would be safe and handy. We fixed an aneroid barometer. We installed the two radios and wired them up temporarily pending Jack's more expert attention. On Friday, 3 August, we had brie and a glass of wine for lunch, by that evening most of the immediate jobs seemed done, and *Swingaway* looked shipshape and comfortable.

We had a visitor, George Jarvis, a colleague I had known in Africa, a keen sailor who had introduced small-boat sailing to Sierra Leone. He stayed for a drink and a talk. I know no better place to relax and yarn than a small boat in harbour. It is almost worth having one simply for this purpose. Close quarters, airy yet warm, everything at hand, no telephone, no TV, an atmosphere of informality, and (for everyone used to the sea) a feeling of being safe and shut-in for a time against wind, waves and weather.

On Saturday I got in food and drink for another party. This time it was to be my two cinema colleagues James and Charles and their wives. Neither of them was a small-boat sailor but Charles was a good photographer and had offered to take photos of *Swingaway* under sail. But to get the right weather, the cameraman in a launch or dinghy, and the yacht with sails just right on various headings, might take several week-ends. There wasn't time to set it all up. However he took some attractive pictures of the boat alongside in the marina. James presented me with a set of Solitaire, an absorbing (and infuriating) game for passing the time when at sea.

The guests left at 4 pm to catch the train and Bob and I tidied up while we waited for Jack, who had not been able to make it for the lunch. He arrived at 9 pm, having come down by train. We planned to leave on Sunday and hoped to be in Teignmouth by Monday night. But the weather report that evening forecast north-west winds Force 6 to 8 backing south-west. On Sunday morning we moved to an outside berth and got the floats out. By now it was blowing hard from the south-west. If I had been on my own I would have got into my bunk with a good book and waited for better weather. But I felt quite strongly that Jack and Bob were raring to go and it would take the edge off their enthusiasm if we started by stopping where we were. Besides, the calendar was moving steadily towards 20 August, when the Teignmouth boat yard would be shut.

So after lunch I took the key of the loo up to the marina office and we left Lymington. We had already got the mainsail half-hoisted while *Swingaway* was alongside, and reefed to about nine inches below the first batten. Out through the narrow channel under the engine, we found stormy yellow water and a short, steep sea over which *Swingaway* bucked and kicked like an unwilling horse. At the entrance Bob and Jack went forward to hoist the reefed main. Somehow it all went wrong. In the wind the burgee halyard which ran up the mast to the cross trees, fouled the main halyard and the whole lot jammed somewhere out of reach. When I left the tiller and the controls for a moment, the engine stalled. There was shoal water to leeward of us.

At the very start of our venture the whole thing could have ended in disaster. It was perhaps a good thing that the three of us were at the very beginning of our acquaintance, and that both of the others were new to small-boat sailing. For neither of them really turned a hair.

'Is it always like this?' enquired Bob with gung-ho innocence.

And Jack, quiet no doubt because of ingrained Navy discipline, later produced cups of coffee, telling us: 'I've put a tot of rum in.'

Fortunately the working jib was ready hanked on and hoisting it we got clear into deeper water. The wind was screaming in the rigging and the Solent was a mass of white water. With the main halyard jammed and the engine out, there was no thought of beating through the Needles. We could make Newtown River under jib alone and I kept her going as close to the wind as I could. With the wind Force 7 or better we fairly tore along and once in the shelter of the Island the sea smoothed out somewhat. Though it was a Sunday in August we had the world to ourselves. Those with any sense were at home watching television. We managed to get the engine started, to take us in, but it sounded very noisy. The storm had broken some blades of the wind generator, as I was taking it out of its socket. It was going at such a furious rate as to shake the steel railing, and I thought it might disintegrate or jump overboard. Also the waves had torn part of the rubbing-strake off the starboard float. I cut it loose and stowed it, to be screwed back later. At least if we were no nearer Teignmouth, we were not much farther away. We had a sheltered anchorage. And we were able to disentangle the main halyard and carry the flag halyard away from the mast so it never fouled again.

The wind blew all night, gusting to Force 10, but during the morning seemed to moderate somewhat. If one wants to get going it is easy to be persuaded that a temporary lull is going to last. The 0630 report forecast gales in the Portland/Plymouth area. At 1355 they predicted Force 8 winds in the Wight area 'at first'. That sounded more promising, the tide was going east and we decided to leave. Bob and Jack were cheerful, both having had a good night, and they wanted to carry on if possible. If it was too bad we could put into Yarmouth. The engine refused to start and eventually we had to get out under sail. I tried the main alone but she would not manoeuvre and we had to go down river under reefed main and storm jib. I never could get *Swingaway* to tack to windward or even go on a close reach under one sail alone. We tacked across to Lymington and back to Yarmouth then down Channel to the Needles. In the Solent a short race in the Admiral's Cup series was abandoned. The big yachts, carrying scraps of sail, turned and went back to Cowes. We ploughed on, however, climbing over endless mountains of water whipped by the wind. We decided to carry on until the 1800 weather forecast.

By then we were out in the open sea and the switchback water, caused by the wind against tide, gave way to longer, deeper waves. The forecast was Force 6 to 8 gales 'moderating later'. Our wind gauge measured winds from 34 to 50 knots. Even with the little canvas we had set, *Swingaway* was doing 5 to 6 knots. There was continual spray and some solid water, all over the boat and in the cockpit, and everything and everybody was soaking wet. All day there was bright sunshine and a cloudless sky to the west but overhead an arch of white cloud, what Bob told us is called in New Zealand a 'nor'west arch'. Here no doubt was a 'sou'west arch' and an accompaniment to the heavy sou'wester of the Channel as the other one is to the Southerly Buster of the Tasman Sea.

We tacked up towards Bournemouth, then south on the starboard tack. Night came and we went on down to the Anvil Light. A clear, starry sky, Anvil Light, St Catherine's and the loom of Portland Bill lighthouse, all in sight. But a thoroughly uncomfortable, miserable night all the same. We were shaken about like puppets and violently seasick. Several of the cabin ports and the forrad hatch were leaking and we were deluged with water and soaked whether on deck or below. By 0300 Bob and Jack seemed exhausted, I certainly was, and we hove to. With the sails we had on, but the storm jib backed, she lay fairly comfortably, making way crab-wise out to sea. We stayed hove to for two and a half hours till dawn. There being no other craft nearer than the nearest harbour, we all got our heads down and by full daylight felt infinitely better.

We had made little progress in the night and were to the southwest of St Alban's Head. On the port tack we could point 285 degrees which would bring us to Portland Harbour. It was still blowing hard and we decided to call in there until the weather was definitely better. It would be half way to Teignmouth. I was feeling pleased with the boat. Except for the leaks round the portholes she had stood up to the weather well. We still couldn't get any sign of life from the engine, but Portland was an enormous harbour and we could go in under sail. We passed the Shambles light vessel at noon and went in the northern entrance. There were vacant moorings up near the yacht club and we tacked about trying to come up into the wind with a buoy under the bow. Even reefed as it was the mainsail outbalanced the storm jib, *Swingaway* handled awkwardly and I made several bosh shots. Bob, on one of the floats with a boat-hook, finally caught the eye of a buoy, but before he could get a line through we paid away and, despite letting go the sheets promptly, there was too much wind for him to hold her. Unwilling to let the buoy go he was pulled into the water, lost the boat-hook and began to swim after it. I expect we would have sorted ourselves out eventually, but there was a launch pottering about and she came over and took a line to a buoy for us. First handing us the boat-hook, Bob climbed back on board and cheerfully told us: 'It's just right for a swim'.

Realising the difficulty, neither Bob nor Jack showed any signs of desertion or mutiny or even of assigning blame. Without an engine many multihulls are not easy in harbour. Missing a heavy keel, the faster they are in the open the more they barge about in the stable-yard.

Jack went ashore in the dinghy to send Heather a telegram. Bob eased the centre-board that had somehow jammed, and hung out clothes to dry. I turned in and slept until 1800. The next day we got away in good time with a west wind still against us, but now only Force 4 to 5. It took us on a reach down to the Portland Race. Just as well we had not been there the previous day or the day before that. There was a narrow strip of smooth water not more than a cable-and-a-half and through this, near the shore, a motor-boat was making its way. With the wind against us and still no engine, we had to tack out and as soon as we crossed the line of calm water, like running into a hostile crowd, the boat was seized and shaken, tossed this way and that by the confused sea. It took us an uncomfortable hour to beat round the Bill and head up towards Lyme Regis and Beer Head. The Portland Race is rightly respected and avoided by yachtsmen.

By 1800 there was land ahead that looked like the Ness, a wooded headland to the south of Teignmouth. At night it was floodlit and looked most picturesque. In one of the pubs ashore there was an old photo of the Ness and below it the wreck of a schooner driven ashore in a storm at the turn of the century. All but one of the crew had been saved by a local lifeboat. The entrance to Teignmouth is not easy and our *Pilot to the South Coast Harbours*, advised that 'the sands on the bar are constantly shifting. Without a pilot or assistance from local fishermen or boat-owners, the entrance should not be attempted by strangers, except with the utmost care in settled weather'. So, especially without an engine, we decided to anchor outside. Going carefully by the chart we came in to land to the east of the pier and let go anchor at 2000 in 8 feet. With a moderating offshore breeze we spent a comfortable, uneventful night.

In the morning Bob went ashore in the dinghy to find Honnor Marine's yard and ask them to help us in. John Westell was away but had left word for them to expect us. In about half-an-hour Bob came rowing back and at the same time a launch came out of the entrance just to the south of us. They gave us a line, towed us in and took us to a fore-and-aft mooring at the side of the main channel, just off Honnor Marine's yard. Instead of arriving on Monday as I had hoped, it was now Thursday morning.

So far as we three crew were concerned I don't think setting out in a storm had done any harm. In fact it had brought us closer together and made each of us feel he could rely on the others in an emergency. From being three individuals we had become a team.

7
A Needle to an Anchor

THE first thing was to have the engine looked at. The yard had no mechanic but they highly recommended one working in a shed next door. Before lunch the man in charge, Don, as I knew him, came out to have a look. Busy with other jobs I let him get on with it. Until there came a quiet voice: 'Here, come and have a look at this.' Don would have made a good actor. He didn't raise his voice: he had no need to. The drama was there in what anybody could see – in what I saw as I gazed horrified at the engine. He had taken the plugs out and as the boat rocked slightly at her moorings, water welled up in the holes. I can see it still. The engine was literally full of sea water. I suppose you could say as far as engines are concerned it was a fate worse than death.

It had all stemmed from the survey report. Renewing the bearing had led to breaking the exhaust pipe. The new exhaust pipe had not had enough upward curve. The pitching of the boat in the storm (we had been up and down like a rocking-horse) had filled the exhaust and then the engine.

'It'll have to be taken right down,' he said. 'You want a new exhaust. There isn't enough slope in that one.'

'How soon you can do it?'

'We'll do the best we can.'

'How much?'

'Hm-m . . . About a hundred pounds – that is for labour.'

'You'd better go ahead then.'

There was really no choice. After lunch three of them came on board and in an hour they had everything disconnected (with all the loose pipes and wires it looked like a heart transplant), the engine hoisted out into a work-boat and taken ashore.

Heather had come and picked up Jack and they were staying ashore with his parents. I took the train up to London that evening. With me in a bag I had the ship's compass. There were some bubbles in it and I thought it had better go back to the makers, Browne of Leadenhall Street. Bob stayed on board. He had given up his pad in London and *Swingaway* was now his home.

Up in London I spent Friday first in the City getting charts, most of which had been ordered. I tried to strike a middle path between having charts that we found unnecessary and, the other way, badly needing charts we didn't have. At least an ocean voyage doesn't need so much documentation as a coastal cruise calling at many ports. The cost of charts keeps going up and it is difficult and expensive to get them corrected for long. To get Notices to Mariners and correct them yourself is beyond the average yachtsman. It is a full-time job. Fortunately small boats can get by easier than large ones and navigation is an art depending on all kinds of information – including eyes and ears. For this voyage I got *Portsmouth to the Canaries, North Atlantic Ocean Eastern Portion, Consol Lattice Chart Portsmouth to Canaries* (we tried to use it but didn't have much success – it is tricky counting all those dots and dashes) *Ria de Vigo* (just in case), *Bay of Biscay, Gran Canaria to Hierro.* For the next section I got *South Atlantic Ocean Eastern Portion* (as we got nearly to South America the *Western Portion* would have been useful – at one point we went over the edge of the chart, which was disconcerting), *Routeing Chart South Atlantic September* (fascinating and useful for planning, based on average winds over the years), *Cap Vert to Cap de Naze Dakar, Ascension Island* (just in case), *St Helena* (just in case), *Orange River to Cape of Good Hope, Table Bay to Cape Agulhas, Table Bay.* In addition I got *Indian Ocean, Routeing Chart Indian Ocean November, Australia Southern Portion, Approaches to Rotnet Island, Champion Bay to Cape Naturalist* and a few more covering *Eastern Australia and New Zealand.* I divided my shopping between Potters and Kelvin Hughes, then conveniently situated opposite one another in the Minories, though now Potters have become part of the firm opposite. In addition I got several plotting sheets which were cheap and proved useful. They allow room to set out a sight, for which most ocean charts are not big enough.

Then I went on to the compass makers, who looked at the Sestrel and said it badly needed attention. Besides the bubbles, the gimbals were out of true. They thought they might be able to have it ready by next Friday, but I was to telephone on Monday to confirm. On Saturday I had a swim in the local baths in the morning (I was trying to keep fit). On Sunday I had a last walk through the wood and over the fields along the Mole River to the west of Box Hill. It is one of the best parts of the valley, the sun shone, and I could hardly have had a better last look (so to speak) at the land. One should follow Houseman's advice: 'Look thy last on all things lovely, every hour . . . ' But not many live so intensely and I generally appreciate good things most when leaving them for a long time – or when coming back to them. In the afternoon I drove down to Teignmouth, arriving about 8 pm.

All the riverside sheds and workyards being shut on Sunday evening, it cost me a search to find my way down an alley to the water, and some hearty hulloaing to raise Bob. However he finally heard and rowed over to collect me in the dinghy. It was only perhaps 50 yards out to *Swingaway*, but when the tide was running out combined with the river current, it was as much as one could do to stem it. Either one had to point upstream rowing furiously and making crabwise progress, or else start from a point so far above the yacht that there was time to pull out before being carried past. We got proficient at rowing ourselves and one another, but with visitors, especially ladies, it was more hazardous. We used to counteract the effects of external wetting by the internal warmth of a *Swingaway* gin fizz. Perhaps I should give the recipe: 1 part gin, 2 parts dry vermouth, 1 part mixed orange and lemon juice, angostura bitters, soda water to taste.

Bob had been enjoying himself, exploring the river in the dinghy, and the surrounding hills on foot. He had also been doing some jobs. He had refixed the rubbing-strake that had been torn off the float in the storm. He had put foam rubber round the forward hatch-cover to stop it leaking. He had started to re-cement round the ports in the cabin, again to stop any leaks. There was no news of the engine and with a gaping hole in the cockpit one was very conscious of its absence. We sat round a fish-and-chip supper by the light of the Tilley lamp and discussed all we had to do or get done. Jack hadn't been on board. Presumably he and Heather were enjoying themselves at his parents' place and looking up old friends.

It was to be a busy week. On Monday Bob went on with the windows. I went ashore, had a talk to the mechanic and saw the engine already clear of salt water and ready for reassembly. It had not suffered any permanent damage or corrosion and he reckoned he would have it back on the boat within a week. At high tide I had a swim and took the opportunity to have a look at the bottom. Somehow we seemed to have collected patches of weed. It would be advisable to beach her, scrub her down and put on another coat of anti-fouling. There was some local shopping to do – a tool-box, a container for paraffin, some fresh food, beer for Bob. From the yard office I rang London about the compass – they would have it ready by Friday afternoon and it would be about £14. I rang the wind generator people, who promised to put some spare blades in the post. On the phone I got talking about generating electricity on a long voyage, and the man I was talking to suggested we should connect the propeller shaft to the alternator, so by putting the engine in neutral when sailing the turning of the propeller would work the alternator. We didn't get round to it, but there seems no reason why it wouldn't work provided there was enough drive from the propeller and the gearing was arranged to drive the alternator fast enough.

After lunch John Westell and the head of the yard came on board and spent an hour looking at the boat, testing the girders to the floats and their attachments, inspecting the rigging, looking at the hull. They decided she was in good trim, but they offered the services of the yard for any work or spares we wanted before we left. They would come and have another look when we were loaded up and before we left. As for cleaning the bottom, we could let the boat dry out between tides just outside their shed, opposite where we were lying.

We made friends with workmen in the yard. The chaps working on the engine came and fished during their lunch break and on the rising tide. Some of them plunged in for a swim as we did ourselves. We fed well on local fish and a particularly luscious lardy-cake from one of the cake shops. The piles of the rickety jetties nearby were thick with enormous mussels. Grilled with butter or as *moules marinières* they were delicious.

On Tuesday Jack appeared and set to work on the Sailor radio. *Swingaway*'s backstay had large insulators spliced into it, one at the top and at the bottom, so it could be used as a wireless aerial. He fixed a lead from the backstay to the radio in the cabin and spent a long time trying out stations both on the main set and on the hand-held direction-finder. As soon as he switched to direction-finding there was a big loss of power and I think the length of the ferrite rods was the limiting factor. 'I can't get much here,' he said. 'It should be better at sea.'

We discussed at length and on several occasions what food we would take. It might have been the most important aspect of the voyage. Perhaps it was. Jack recommended shopping at a wholesale cash-and-carry store, Normans, near Budleigh Salterton. On Tuesday afternoon we were to drive over and have a look. We had made out a provisional list of tinned meat, fish, vegetables, fruit, plus rice, oatmeal, sugar, dried milk, sauces, jams, oil, margarine, squash. We didn't know what we would be able to get *en route* and in any case were calling at few ports, so we wanted enough for two or three months. We were to go in two cars and Jack would lead the way; but when the time came Jack couldn't find Heather who had been left on the beach, so Bob and I set out, and he was to catch us up at the shop. We were to go on to his parents for supper and it was just near-by.

We found Normans and wandered round. There was plenty of choice and the prices were low. We could have stocked up then and there but thought we ought all three to be agreed, so just went round noting names and prices. By closing time there was still no sign of Heather and Jack so we drove on to Jack's parents and introduced ourselves, welcomed by an effusive collie dog. Jack's father was knowledgeable and enthusiastic about local history and especially the palmy days of Budleigh Salterton when it was a thriving port. 'It gradually silted up and they let it go,' he told us. 'It could easily be reopened. It was as good a port as any in the West Country.' Jack arrived after we had had a cuppa and Jack's mother was in the kitchen preparing an enormous high tea, but Heather didn't join us until much later, more than half-way through the meal. Jack too knew his local history and had read a lot on the subject of King Arthur and related archaeology. We drank a local beer with the meal, but the talk got on to cider, and Jack's father insisted on going part way back with us later in the evening, and taking us to a pub with 'the best cider in the district'. It really was something special, strong and mellow, and we sat there until closing time, made warm-hearted and convivial by a nectar that could have been distilled from celestial golden apples.

I never knew why Jack hadn't come shopping with us as arranged, or why he and Heather had arrived separately and so late. It seemed there must have been some misunderstanding or disagreement, but nothing was said by either of them and it was no occasion to enquire. Neither then nor later did Jack talk about his family, and indeed during the cruise we talked hardly at all about our private, personal lives. We were too busy sailing the boat.

On Wednesday we had arranged with the yard to beach *Swingaway*. Since we had no engine they came out with a launch shortly after 0800 when the tide was full and towed us over until the bow was touching the door of an enormous corrugated-iron shed. By 1000 we had started scrubbing down the bottom and by noon we started the painting. Jack joined us in the morning and the three of us worked flat out to get it done. Jack's parents arrived with some friends to see the boat at lunch time. They had to pick their way over a jumble of seaweed, sand, stones, and the timber and iron of an old slipway. The boat was a muddle inside and in our paint-stained clothes we could only knock off for a short time to snatch a quick drink and a sandwich. However, Jack fixed a ladder for them to get on board and have a look, and they promised to come back for a proper visit before we sailed.

During the day a boat came round from the mechanic's yard with the engine. They unloaded it slung on a pole at the water's edge and, using ropes, got it hoisted on board. Bob helped them with a bit of rugby muscle. Thereafter, while we were slapping on the jelly-like antifouling underneath the boat, they were tapping and tramping up above. The painting seemed to go on and on, even though we had Jack to help us. At one point it seemed doubtful if we would have enough anti-fouling, and then if we would beat the rapidly-rising tide. In the end everything fell into place and by 1600 we were cleared away and waiting for the boat to float off.

By this time I was limping. I had been wearing a pair of rubber-soled canvas shoes and had trodden on a rusty nail after lunch. It was sticking up out of an old baulk of timber, half rusted away, and without thinking, as if I had been wearing stronger shoes, I stamped down on it to bend it over and make it safe. But I did it so hurriedly and carelessly that I came down vertically on the point and it still had enough strength to drive through the shoe and into my foot. I cleaned and taped it as well as I could, but going through the thick skin of the sole it was a shut-in wound, there was little bleeding, and by that night it was swollen, sore and clearly infected. I had already handed in my medical card, as required, and the nearest doctor I knew was in London. However we had a good supply of medicines for the cruise which included penicillin, two of the sulpha drugs, morphine injections etc. There was still a lot to do, I had to make a rush trip to London, and we wanted to get away early next week when the boatyard closed. I thought this justified treating myself rather than spend half a day in a local hospital. I began a course of penicillin, kept the wound open and squeezed out any pus. In two days the inflammation was under control and in a week it had healed cleanly. Jack objected we should keep the drugs for use at sea, but I pointed out there was still enough to treat an army, and if I had gone to see a doctor, besides spending valuable time, I might have been told not to go until it was better.

We spent Wednesday night tied up outside the shed, and on Thursday morning, the yard launch being engaged, we got back to our mooring by rowing over to the buoys with a rope and warping the yacht across. While we were doing it a work-boat came down at a spanking pace inside the line of buoys, and despite our shouts, ran into the rope. It was as much his fault as ours, but there was no harm done and after some cursing he went off amiably enough. I was to catch the train to London that night leaving my car for Bob and Jack to get the provisions – we had made out a list – and also duty-free beer, wine and spirits from Plymouth, the nearest supplier. I had made the arrangement with the Customs and placed the order. We were to share the cost, but I left enough to pay initially. Altogether we spent about £87 on food and £19 on drink. With another £24 at Las Palmas it was more than enough to see us to Cape Town over a period not far short of three months.

Bob and Jack left late in the morning and I met old friends, Stella and Frank from Totnes, who came on board for a drink before lunch. They admired the boat and we sat chatting until there was only just time to get ashore for a restaurant meal, not having had time to get anything for lunch on board. After we said goodbye late in the afternoon, I lugged an empty gas cylinder along to a refill depot, and tried to get information about supplies on our route. We set out with one calor-gas container in use and three spares, getting one refill in Las Palmas and arriving after three months with one still in hand.

At 6 pm I walked to the station to get the London train, and arrived in town late that evening. Britain isn't quite as broad as it's long, but the West Country is far enough away to be as much a distant country as Scotland. My most important job on Friday was to collect the compass. I climbed up to the shop on the 'deck' of the P-&-O building in the City about 3.30 pm. The man I had dealt with wasn't there, and after another man had looked about, it was clear the compass wasn't there either.

'I'll ask the factory,' he told me, and got on to the telephone. 'They're still testing it,' he explained after a short talk, 'but it'll be ready on Monday.'

'That's no good,' I replied, 'we're sailing on Monday. On a long voyage. It's only the compass that's holding us up.'

'Perhaps you'd like to talk to them.' He held out the receiver.

'We have to test it for sub-zero temperatures and for tropical conditions.' The voice over the phone sounded as level as the bottom of a graph. 'The work's done. But it ought to be tested. It's going into the fridge now.'

I didn't think we'd be in sub-zero temperatures and we could take a chance on the tropics. We wouldn't be in the Sahara. I wasn't coming up to London again. I told the man in the shop and he had another talk to the factory.

'We can send a messenger for it.'

I can't remember exactly but it was somewhere like Enfield.

'Can you come back at five o'clock? We close then but there'll be somebody until late and you can sit in here if the messenger's held up.'

I was back at 4.45. The messenger hadn't arrived but he was on his way. By 5.30 I had the compass. It looked like a new instrument and in spite of the trouble, I felt it had been worthwhile.

On Saturday morning I went down to Teignmouth by train and went on board *Swingaway* with the compass and the rest of my gear. The boat was loaded down to the gunnels and what with the food, gallons of water and extra petrol and paraffin, every corner seemed crammed with small tins, plastic containers and large cans. You could see she was lower in the water.

John Westell came on board and had a last look round. 'She'll lose a bit of speed,' he said, 'but it won't matter . You'll be getting lighter all the time.'

I fixed up the yard's bill which came to £70 including mooring, towing in, use of the slip, telephone, antifouling, and a few spares, the most expensive item being a length of heavy stainless-steel rigging that we never used. I doubt if we could have set it up. Most useful was a supply of thick rubber rings that made the bolts holding the float girders really tight, as several of the fixings got loose and started clicking over the weeks at sea.

The liquor was also on board and had been sealed by the Customs, but Bob had managed to put a couple of bottles aside and they would help our farewells as other stocks were running low. After all we weren't going to get away on Monday, as the engine was not finished. It still had to be tried out. The third exhaust had a very high bend like a croquet-hoop near the engine though it seems to me a bend is more effective the nearer it can be put to the stern. However this one never let in any sea water, though we took the added precaution of hammering a wooden stopper into the exhaust when the engine was not running.

We were now nearly ready to go. Jack's parents came on board for lunch, bringing sandwiches with them despite instructions. To start we had *moules marinières* and Bob produced *ananas flambés au rhum* to follow. Again we sat round talking until late afternoon. Most of the work was done and I spent the evening sending off last postcards and letters.

On Monday Don came on board and gave the last touches to the engine. He started it up at 1100 and we left it running for nearly two hours to give it a good test and charge the batteries. In the evenings we had been using paraffin lamps; now we had the luxury of electric light. At the last minute we remembered brushes and paint we had left in Honnor Marine's yard and, with the yard closed for their holiday, we managed like thieves to get in from Don's premises through a connecting door. The whole place was shut up and dead, with dark tide water lapping under the huge doors of the launching shed – an ideal setting for the ghosts of ancient mariners. But I was too full of anticipation for it to give me any bad dreams.

We got bread on board – ten large loaves to see us to Las Palmas. We weren't going to bake and when the bread was done we would eat biscuits. We got some fresh meat – chops and sausages. We already had 30lbs of potatoes, 5 dozen oranges, 10lbs of apples, a lot of bacon and ham, 5 dozen eggs, some dipped in boiling water and some in isinglass to preserve them. We also had an enormous piece of Rumanian 'cheddar' cheese. I nipped into a shop and bought eight large slabs of chocolate which I kept in a secret store, producing them on occasions of disaster or celebration as a morale and energy booster. For a more regular sweet ration we had a great jar of boiled sweets.

Tuesday dawned overcast, grey and chilly. There was a thin drizzle of rain. The shipping forecast gave winds variable Force 2 to 3. The barometer showed 1031 millibars. My watch was 61 seconds slow on GMT and losing about seven seconds a day. We had a mishap at the very outset. Bob was casting off forrad while I was at the helm and the engine controls when the line to the upstream buoy, instead of slipping freely through the ring, jammed. Again Bob went into the water and this time lost his glasses. It was out of the question to try and recover them as there were a good two or three fathoms of not-clear water and a tide running out which would carry them away from the buoy. At least he had another pair. Our second attempt at casting off was more successful and we slipped down river and out of the mouth under the engine. Outside there was a light east wind and we hoisted the main and large genoa, at first a point free, then on a reach as we made some offing.

In the drizzle on the esplanade were three figures waving. They were Jack's parents and Heather come to see him off.

Part Two
THE CRUISE

NOVEMBER — Saturday **3**

Day 57
7758
3037
4721

(307-58) Week 44

Bar. — 1024   Watch — no check
— Wind stayed moderate in night. Cloud & stars. We are now short of electricity.
— No wind generator for some days & no engine, so 12 volt batteries are down. Will have to use Tilly Lamps & dry cell batteries as much as possible.
— <u>Centreboard</u> all up = 20 turns.
— Wind veered to West - astern. Running under mainsail & heavy genoa "goosewinged" on starboard side. 3-5 kts. Bright, fresh day. Radio Cape Town says, light to moderate winds.
— Morning sight gives (azimuth 93°) 13° 08.6 (E)
LOG. 7758. (in trip. 4721)   Lowered main
                              running under genoa
1100 GMT. Wind increased & veered more North. (more sea)
Watch 1m 35s. slow on GMT. (recently good)
Mer. Passage. Gives Lat 33° 54' South. with long B.F. gives fix. 13° 30 E. Run say. log. 96 miles. about 250 miles to Cape Town *
— Wind more North. Running 120° on port tack under genoa × 5 knots. Strong following wind.
1500 GMT. Watch 1m 36 sec. slow (recently good)
— <u>Pumped bilges</u> 110 strokes.
— In evening wind strong, decided to heave to & lie ahull for night. in view of no compass light & failing batteries (no engine). Very warm & slept well.

Page from the ship's log. Day 57; 3rd. November.

8
THE HARBOUR CLEARED

We passed Hope's Nose and then Berry Head doing about 5 knots, and then at 1300 rounded Start Point. From Start Point we took our departure on a course of 250° magnetic, and streamed the Walker log set at zero. The wind stayed easterly and we set the spinnaker. The rain cleared away and we jogged comfortably down the Channel with a light following breeze.

I suppose our last sight of England ought to have been a dramatic moment. Like every schoolboy I had learned to recite the immortal lines: 'And like an eagle free/Away the good ship flies, and leaves/Old England on the lee'. But we were all too busy below and about the boat, stowing stores and gear and checking everything — now in use — to think of Cunningham's poem. All the same there was a lot of satisfaction about and I looked up contentedly at our 'gallant mast' and the Red Ensign which we flew for a spell on the after-stay.

We ran the engine for a routine half-hour and put back the wooden bung in the stern. Before nightfall we lowered the spinnaker and set watches — three hours each starting at 2200 and ending at 0700. The first night Jack took the evening watch, I took the middle and Bob the morning, and each subsequent night we moved one on. Alternating like this we kept the night watches up for the whole voyage.

During my watch the skies cleared and the moon came out about half-full. As usual in the Channel there was a lot of shipping, and one cargo boat came close — too close. I did see her in good time on the starboard bow, gave way and put the helm up. But all the same she passed within 50 yards, always a nasty experience. No question in these encounters of maintaining one's right of way. Perhaps it was a good thing I had the middle watch. Jack, knowing the rule of the road ('power driven vessels must keep out of the way of sailing vessels') might have taken it literally; Bob might not have reacted quickly enough. Shipping at night is always a hazard for yachts. On cargo-boats, even with radar, there is always the human factor of inattention or fatigue and, indeed, the practical factor of their speed and slowness in altering course. Our night watches were not always so fraught. Sometimes it was good to be alone with the luminous outline of the log trailing astern and the glow of the compass-light for sole company.

At least we were on our way with a fair wind. I felt elated and a sense of fulfilment just in the fact of having set out after so much preparation and so many delays. *Swingaway* was going along easily and I held the tiller (with the wind on the quarter the self-steering was unreliable) and kept a sharp look out all round until it was 0400 and time to call Bob. As usual he was sound asleep and took a little waking but once aroused came on watch in quick time. Besides the navigation lights which came off the batteries, we kept a Tilley lamp burning through the night and sometimes put the main cabin lights on when coming on or going off watch. For chartwork at night there was a good concentrated electric light on a flexible metal stalk just over the chart table.

By 0800 the second day there were 93 miles on the log. The wind still held from the east. I took a first morning sight and somehow got the longitude five degrees in error – a mere 300 miles! It meant we were in the Seine, somewhere near Rouen Cathedral! However a noon sight tallied with our dead reckoning and with a radio fix. Thereafter my sights got more reliable with practice. There were occasions when the horizon was hazy or the boat was trying to stand on its head, and I knew the readings were subject to error. But the result generally reflected only the few miles error one might have expected by being a few minutes out on the sextant.

Jack was having his own problems with the radios. There was a lot of interference and difficulty in locating stations. At noon with 118 miles on the log we altered course a few degrees further south to 230° magnetic. At the same time we found the centre-board had jammed. When we dismantled it, we found the worm-and-gear assembly had broken. A cast-iron metal lug which held the worm in place had broken off; as a result the worm was turning out of place and jamming against a large metal washer instead of moving the cog which raised and lowered the centre-board. We could at a pinch work it by hand, but without welding equipment there was no possibility of a proper repair. There was not likely to be much windward work on our passage to the Canaries but we would have to get it repaired there, because of the head winds on the next leg.

In the afternoon Bob and I had our first bathe, soon to become a daily routine. Jack like a true sailor held off for a while, but soon joined us when the weather and the water got warmer. We always trailed a rope, and there were some days when the boat was travelling too fast even for a dip, but otherwise we swam or trailed through the water without misgiving and without mishap. In a trimaran the spaces between the floats and the main hull form enclosures in the sea. They may be more a psychological than an actual protection, but it is likely that the disturbance of the water and the presence of the floats would confuse or deter a predator. We saw sharks several times and they didn't stop us bathing, though we never happened to be in the water when they were actually in view.

At evening the wind from the east died away and an hour or so later a light breeze came from the west, and held through the night at Force 3 to 4. Then the third day at sea it freed to the north and gradually died. We set the spinnaker then lowered it when the wind drew ahead. All day we made only 30 miles. But at 0930 radio bearings on Round Island in the Scillies, Ushant, Isle de Seine and Lugo, gave us 7° west longitude and 47° 50′ north. At least we had made a good offing and were well clear of Ushant.

I am recording a lot of round-the-compass-clock steering directions, but courses and fine adjustments are central to sail as opposed to steam. Some courses are a compromise between where *you* want to go and where those innocent, puffing-cheeked cherubs (declared by Charles Lamb to have no bottoms – innocent indeed) want you to go. Therein lies the skill of sailing, and a hand on the tiller can be as delicate as a musician's. A soldier's wind is one from behind that drives you willy-nilly toward your goal. By contrast motor-ships like motor-cars drive round the world on M1-like shipping lanes. At the extreme I believe it takes lumbering oil-tankers half-a-mile to change course at all.

That evening as on other evenings to follow, there was a glorious sunset. There were amber and purple nimbus clouds all round the horizon. They piled up like pillars of a temple high above the level sea. The peace and majesty of these evenings made up for days of storm, setbacks and discomforts. The scale of sea and sky dwarfed the boat to a crawling insect, a speck, a nothing. At the time there was no need of anything more. It was enough to sit and gaze and gaze. The dawns were beautiful too, but somehow it was at evening we sat and drank it in with most enjoyment. Dawn came as a relief after long nights of watching, but there was that grey, cold prelude to the sun. And the mood was different. The day with its work lay ahead. There was urgency and un-repose. At evening there was more expansiveness and relaxed ease.

Always as we went south there was dawn on our left hand and sunset on our right. You grew so accustomed to it that it was like a familiar landscape – the view from the kitchen window, the picture over the mantelpiece, the garden from the back door. It was the same with the sea. It was like a country scene in different seasons and weathers. We saw it stretching ahead or following behind us. We looked down into it lying on deck, or watched it hurrying past the gunnel. Its patterns, its waves, its spray, its frothy eddies, formed the hills and valleys, the woods and meadows of our watery terrain. It spoke to us in different voices through the day. In the cabin it was the world outside. And at night it lulled us to sleep or sometimes kept us awake with its crashing and banging.

That night there was little wind and we drifted through the darkness with the lights of Biscay fishing boats for company. In the morning one of them came close by us. It was a strange craft unlike our stubby British trawlers, with high, flared bows and with the trawl-net towing from wide arms stretching from the boat at an upward angle almost like great fishing-rods. Now we were in a dead calm and for two hours in the morning motored through a glassy sea, not so much because of the distance covered as to relieve the monotony. In the afternoon two triangular fins appeared off the port bow. These were sharks come like tax-officials to inspect us – or should I say muggers of the sea? In either case they were no friends, and we put out a shark hook on a transparent line baited with sausage. We got no bites. Perhaps it was just as well. They might have been too much for us. At least the sharks brought a breeze and for a time we did four knots under main and spinnaker. By 2030 that evening there were 300 miles on the log.

By the fifth day at sea we were in longitude 8° 50′ west and latitude 45° 57′ north, steering 210° to clear Cape Finisterre, the Spanish Land's End. During the day the wind freshened from the south-west and for a time after lunch we could only steer 190′ which would have landed us at La Coruña with the tedious prospect of beating west without full use of the centreboard. Fortunately the wind freed again soon to the west, and we sauntered on, still at no better than four knots, but once again on course. The BBC forecast gave northerly winds in the Biscay-Finisterre area.

We noticed the Walker log had stopped registering. Hauling it in we found that though we were a hundred miles from land, a piece of plastic wrapping had caught round it. The development of plastics as fibreglass, nylon, Terylene, Plexiglass, Formica, Bakelite and the rest, has brought a revolution to yachting. What once was subject to insect or worm attack, rust and rot, is now immune. The problem of plastic rubbish extends to the sea. Along the shore, floating on the waves or at the bottom of the ocean, plastic rubbish piles up, blows with the wind, drifts with the current. Halfway between Cape Town and Rio, a thousand miles from land, the only two signs of civilisation were a floating door and a plastic bottle.

The morning and noon sight on the sixth day gave us 9° 57′ west, 44° 10′ north. We would clear Finisterre comfortably by 50 miles or so. It was a fine sunny afternoon and by evening there were 466 miles on the log. Except for our slow progress, we were all enjoying this spell of good weather. The sea was our world, this time with its tender, gay, lyrical moods instead of those of anger and violence. We had been gently introduced to the waves. Instead of the headaches and malaise of initial seasickness, we had got our sea legs without upset. We swam every day and ate our way through the fresh food with the zest of open-air appetites.

We ate together all the time, there always seemed to be something to talk about and we took turns at cooking, washing up and routine chores. We all did our own laundry and Jack was the most expert. Taking infinite pains he produced creaseless, spotless shirts, jerseys, trousers, and sometimes had drying garments stretched out all over the fore decks. Bob read more and started studying navigation. When the wind was light we all had more time and on watch I consoled myself for our slow progress with the castles, towers and churches of cloud architecture.

After the fishing boats there were occasional passing ships for company, a freighter going south, a container ship, a tanker going north. For other company we had the gulls that came, flew round the boat and went. Soaring and dipping, skimming the waves, they hardly moved their wings until with a sudden braking movement they would hold them high, flat against the wind, settle on the water then, with a self-conscious, self-satisfied shrug, fold them away until the next flight. Sometimes they would follow the boat and snatch a few scraps. But the pickings were not very rich, for with our own hearty appetites, limited stock, and thousands of miles ahead, we wasted nothing.

On the sixth day the engine began to give trouble, stalling at low revs. Bob was honorary engineer and spent an hour on it, then getting nowhere, decided, as it was Sunday, to postpone further investigation until the start of the working week. An hour may seem a long time to get no result but on a moving boat at sea it is infuriatingly difficult to do the simplest mechanical job. Some activities, like writing, reading or simple cooking are not so badly affected (though pouring liquids is a hazard) but handling a spanner or a screwdriver in an awkward position can be dementing. Parts of marine engines always seem to be difficult to get at. Nuts, pins or small parts fall into the bilge or down a crack, or often enough overboard to be lost for ever. A job at sea is likely to take three times as long as it would in port. Fortified by an omelette for breakfast Bob worked all day Monday, changing plugs and cleaning the carburettor, but the engine still ran irregularly, misfired and eventually stalled. We checked the engine oil for seawater but there was no trace.

'I wouldn't make my living as a real motor-mechanic,' Bob confessed.

'At least you've got more patience and better hands than me or Jack,' I said, not wanting to discourage anything.

That was true. Rugby player and all, he could still handle tiny parts with care and precision. Some days later Bob checked the petrol tank and decided there was some sea water in it. This couldn't have got in through the exhaust. We decided it must somehow have got in through the filler cap which was flush with the deck at the side of the cockpit. The copper screw cap had a good thread, but during the storm in the Channel it must have been under water again and again. There was no way to cover the cap, but from then on we made sure the thread was kept thickly coated with grease. As for the water in the tank we decided to drain it when we got to the Canaries. If we had tried to do it at sea we might have lost half our petrol and risked a fire.

We tried to rig up a substitute supply using a can of unwatered petrol from our reserve stock, but after much trial and error had to give up. We had only a short length of tubing and it was difficult to find a place where the can could be securely fixed. Then we found it impossible to regulate the flow. If we put the can on a level with the engine it didn't get enough fuel to keep it going. If we put the can high up on the seat round the cockpit the engine got too much and the carburettor over-flooded. Finally we gave up, decided to go into harbour under sail, and if we got into trouble we would make the best of our stop-go petrol-and-water mixture. As it was, when we reached Las Palmas, we were able to sail in comfortably and drop anchor. But it added one more to my many experiences of engine failure. Give me pure sail any day.

Once past Finisterre we began to move faster and faster as we came into the region of the Portuguese Trades. The change came on the seventh day at sea in glorious blue-and-gold weather. All morning there was a light breeze from the north-west and we were doing some 3 knots, then from 1400 the wind increased to a steady Force 4 from west-nor-west and our speed rose to 5 or 6 knots. At evening there were 522 miles on the log, the wind followed us all night and the next morning freshened to Force 5. By noon it had become a good Force 6 and there were 638 miles on the log. Had we been going north and beating into the wind it would have been that much stronger. There was a big following sea and breaking waves. *Swingaway* began surfing down the crests of the waves with a surge of excitement and foaming white water, and it became a strenuous business after an hour or so at the helm. Once let her stray a few inches and there was a huge weight of water pushing the stern sideways. The more she wandered from a direct line the more the pressure built up until it needed all one's strength to drag her back. It was hard work, but how exhilarating compared with our previous staid progress. If you think of dramatic colour-shots of surfers riding big waves before they break you get the general idea.

In the night the wind had come from the north. Now it was nor' nor' east. We had been running with the main and genoa first on one tack then on the other, steering on average 220°. On the eighth day we altered to 200° compass, on a course that would take us to the Gran Canaria and Las Palmas. With the wind nearly dead aft we goose-winged the jib and boomed it out. Then as the wind got stronger we had to ease down for the night, lowering the jib, reefing the main, and on the starboard tack holding a course of 225° during the dark hours to bring the wind more on the quarter. The ninth day the wind was stronger than ever, up to Force 7 at times, and we had done our best day's run, nearly 170 miles. The constant work at the helm was tiring us mentally as well as physically, and after several gybes we took down the main altogether. We were now doing 5 to 6 knots under the genoa alone; the boat immediately became more comfortable and steering less of a strain. Later in the day we set the working jib flying, on the port side. This was a twin-running rig of a sort but it still required somebody at the tiller.

However, there was no danger of gybing, it gave us another one or two knots, and we were able to carry it through most of that night.

At 0430 in Bob's watch an unusual noise awoke me and I turned out.

'It's the jib,' Bob explained. 'The wind's getting the wrong side and it's twisting and turning.'

I tried to adjust it but the stubborn brute wouldn't set right and I took it down. For the three hours till daylight we altered course to 190°. We were still going steadily at the same surging, surfing speed. The morning sight on the tenth day gave us 12° 52' west and at noon we were 34° 58' north. We set the twin jibs again and tied down the clews to the forward end of the floats. Thus held out, both sails were steadier and easier. We passed a fine-looking Russian liner, white as a swan and with many passengers on board. Jack said it was a cruise ship and those especially favoured by the Government were treated to a holiday on board.

'Besides,' he added, 'they can have a quiet look round at ports of call.'

We got a bearing on Madeira lying about 237° on the starboard bow. We also got the signal of Las Palmas Radio Beacon on the main Sailor set. It was some 500 miles ahead and too weak to come through on the RDF or to give us a bearing. Every day we sighted several ships and again at night, some passing us going north, others overtaking us going south. There was never the same danger of collision as there is in the Channel, and it was cheering to see them, whether close within half a mile or hull down on the horizon. That evening with 1000 miles on the log we felt we had made a good start and were mightily pleased with ourselves. With toasted cheese for lunch (Jack) and curry for supper (Bob), there was an optimstic, cheerful feeling on board.

Bob entertained us with stories told by the Irish labourers he had worked with. Why do people like to tell stories poking fun at themselves? Parsons tell jokes about parsons, the Scots tell stories about Scotsmen, and the Irish tell stories about the Irish.

'There's the one about the Irishman whose blanket wouldn't come up to his chin,' said Bob. 'So he cut a bit off the bottom and sewed it on the top. Then there's the one about the man whose wife fell in the river and who rushed upstream to rescue her. "You're crazy", people told him. "Go downstream." "No, bedad," he replied, "No way. You just don't know my wife." '

Jack countered with a naval story. 'The admiral inspecting the ship came upon a sailor in the barber's shop having his hair cut. "I see you're having your hair cut in working hours," he said. "Please sir, it grew in working hours – sir." "It didn't *all* grow in working hours, my man." "No sir – but please sir, I'm not having it all cut off – sir," replied the sailor.'

Bob then came back with a rugby story. 'At one time a lot of leading Australian Internationals went to Heaven. Saint Peter, impressed, proposed to set up a match against Hell. "If you like," said the Devil. "But we'll win." "How come?" said Saint Peter. "You've only got a few bloody All Blacks down there." "Maybe," said the Devil. "But then we've got all the referees." '

All I could contribute were a couple of quotes about travel. First, Sir Thomas Beecham: 'I have recently been all round the world and have formed a very poor opinion of it.' And second an American wife to her friends: 'Henry wants to take me on a trip round the world but I'd rather go somewhere else.'

There were some minor mishaps. We lost overboard a snap shackle and a wire stop very useful for rigging the two jibs. Then on another day the boat-hook was lost. Going like a train as we were and with sails rigged exclusively for running, there was no possibility of turning and recovering anything. If anyone had gone overboard... When we bathed in the rushing water, we were doubly careful and clung to a heavy line with a loop under the armpits. At the fastest I preferred to scoop up water with a bucket and improvise a shower-bath on deck.

Except for a single shower of rain the weather kept clear, and it was balmy without being too warm. The breeze saw to that. At night we sailed in a sea of stars and the Milky Way spread round the mast like a halo. Venus shone brightest of all, and when we had two sails up she settled at times right between them, dead ahead as if to guide us. The sails themselves spread out like wings and hour after hour the boat flew on like a great bird. With the rush of our passage went an accompaniment of which I never tired, the sound of surging, boiling water. Though it continued day after day, somehow it never became monotonous, wearisome or nerve-racking, perhaps because it meant progress. There was another noise too, most satisfying to listen to – the low sound of the boat as she went well through the water. It sounded like – 'erraump – erraump – erraump', a tramping, trudging noise. It sounded right, it sounded good, and one got used to listening for it and enjoying it, as a driver enjoys the purr of an engine running smoothly.

Again there were minor troubles. One night the compass light failed. In the light of day we checked the connections and got it going again. Three days later the stern light failed but again it was only the bulb loose in its socket and we fixed it the next day. All the navigation lights (port, starboard and stern light) worked off the batteries with a single switch. There was a white mast-head light on a separate switch. These took a lot more current than the compass light, but while we needed the compass light continuously, we switched the navigation lights on only when there were ships in sight. The brightest light on board was the Tilley lamp, kept in the cabin so as not to blind the helmsman and ready to be brought out and waved in an emergency. We had two large, squarish plastic torches and a supply of chunky batteries. These stood up well to the damp and were more reliable in the end than a rubber-covered torch, though the latter was presumably intended to be waterproof. The effect of a strong torch-light shone on the sails is remarkable. A sudden tower of ghostly light seems to shoot up from the sea. It is like no other light at sea though I suppose the watch on a cargo boat might have no idea what it was. Still it must be a useful supplement to other lights.

Before sailing we had had trouble with the belt connecting the engine with the alternator. It had been loose and it had proved difficult to move the alternator to take up the slack. The belt ran hot then frayed and broke. After trying different shapes and sizes, the mechanic got one that seemed to fit, but now after two weeks at sea it was running hot again. All we could do was to keep a careful eye on it. Another frost plug went and we put in a spare. It was the most awkwardly situated and as it was rough when Bob put it in, he got it slightly askew and after only a few days it began to weep and corrode again. Bob tried to take it out and get it in square, but only managed to make it worse. Then I remembered seeing an old tin of liquid for mending leaks in car radiators, in a box of odds and ends. I rummaged through and found it. There was no indication whether it would work with sea water, but we took a chance, got it into the water jacket, and it did the trick. There were no more leaks for the rest of the voyage.

After ten days at sea we found the night watches beginning to tell and we all needed a rest during the day. So far we hadn't arranged any day watches. This worked in the morning when we were all around and one might as well steer as cook, wash, paint, repair or do any other chore. But we found that after lunch we all wanted to get our heads down. So we arranged that whoever had had the middle watch from 0100 to 0400 at night would be free to sleep or read the next afternoon from 1400 to 1800. The other two would be on watch then for two hours each.

The same day we set the twin-running sails I had had made in Lymington. We had tried out other combinations thoroughly and could go back to them if need be. Their main drawback had been that we hadn't been able to use any effective self-steering. The wind vane worked close hauled and on courses up to a beam wind. But it was no use as soon as the wind came on the quarter or further aft. It took some time to get the new twin-running sails set satisfactorily. The two tacks were fixed to deck bolts near the mast with the clews boomed out by the two spinnaker-poles. The sheets led to a block on the forward end of each float, back to another at the after end, and then to the tiller. We got each boom pointing forward slightly and the tiller set amidships. In the end it all balanced, and the self-steering set-up worked for following winds from Force 3 to Force 5. The pull on the tiller was enormous but of course was balanced equally to port and starboard. Surfing down the waves, it was as if a giant hand was holding the helm. It was one that would never tire, for it was the force of the wind itself.

All that day, all night, all the next day and night, and the next day, we ran under the twin red sails. With the following wind more moderate, down to Force 4 and 3, the lines to the tiller worked just as well as in stronger winds. After so many days continuously at the helm, it was like a holiday to be relieved not only of the physical effort of steering, but the mental concentration as well. We were suddenly set free, masters of extra time to do other chores, to read, play games, sleep or simply loll about and look at the sea and the sky. Jack spent hours playing patience. I produced the solitaire James had given me as a parting present and we all enjoyed it. I also had two books of crosswords with answers at the back. I had a rule not to look up the answers except to confirm a clue I'd already solved, but I didn't *always* stick to it. I learned that 'Stormy Atlantic is one scourge of sailors' was CAT O'NINE TAILS (anagram). Also that 'Mating with leading team-worker' was SEXTANT. Bob spent spare time with Shakespeare and I borrowed the book when he didn't want it.

On the twelfth day the sea was down with the wind, there were no white caps and everything was easier. Strong winds, even favourable ones, become tiring if they go on long enough. Early in the morning we got a fix by RDF on Madeira, Porto Santo, Las Palmas and Tenerife, which gave us a course to Las Palmas of 210° compass, and put the distance at about 250 miles. At 1630 there was a strong signal from Las Palmas on the little Sea-Fix, dead ahead. We passed more ships. We had no means of signalling by day, but Jack had tried to call several ships up after dark, using a small torch with a signalling switch. It wasn't ideal but an Aldis lamp would have been too bulky and too heavy on the batteries. Several times he got no reply, but on the eleventh day he got the name and a message we couldn't follow from a Spanish trawler. On the twelfth day at 2240 he called up a Swedish ship. They replied in English with a lamp like a searchlight, said they had come from Freetown and when he asked them how far it was to Las Palmas and in what direction, replied 'One hundred miles' and 'You are on the right course'.

This was puzzling since our morning radio fix (which agreed with the sun sights) had put us 250 miles from the Gran Canaria, and we had not done 150 miles since then. The exchange had taken some time and they were too far away for any clarification. Jack assured us there was no doubt about the signal and we were ready to believe such good news. We were doing better than a hundred miles a day, and reckoned to reach the Island by the evening of the next day, our thirteenth day at sea and 2nd September. We ought to reach the harbour entrance on the east side of the Island a few hours later and probably heave to and wait for daylight to go in.

All the next day we got ready and looked forward to reaching port. The morning sight gave 14° 48′ west and at noon for the latitude I solemnly, and idiotically, wrote down 28° 90′ north. (As there are only 60 minutes to a degree, this is like an accountant writing £28.150p.) During the day our radio direction-finding suffered a setback as the Sea-Fix broke down. The selector switch failed and when we opened the case, a metal ball like a ball-bearing fell out. Working on a spring it gave the different connections, and it was impossible to repair. We would have to try Las Palmas or post it back to England. It was the handiest of the three direction-finders and gave the clearest signal so this was a real blow. Again there were ships in sight and at 1400 crossing our course from east to west there was a cargo boat being towed by an ocean-going tug. Presumably she had broken down somewhere out in the Atlantic.

We had steak-and-kidney pudding for supper, one of our better meals. The bosom-shaped tins, stacked in pairs as they were, gave rise to the usual comments. 'Tits again,' said Jack, stuffing two of

The crew, Ralph, Bob and Jack. (from left)

Beam wind in Biscay. The controversial kicking-strap wire goes from mast to boom.

Our sailmaker Jack, threading a needle.

Trying out a forward bunk. (see page 89)   Bob firmly on the bosun's chair.

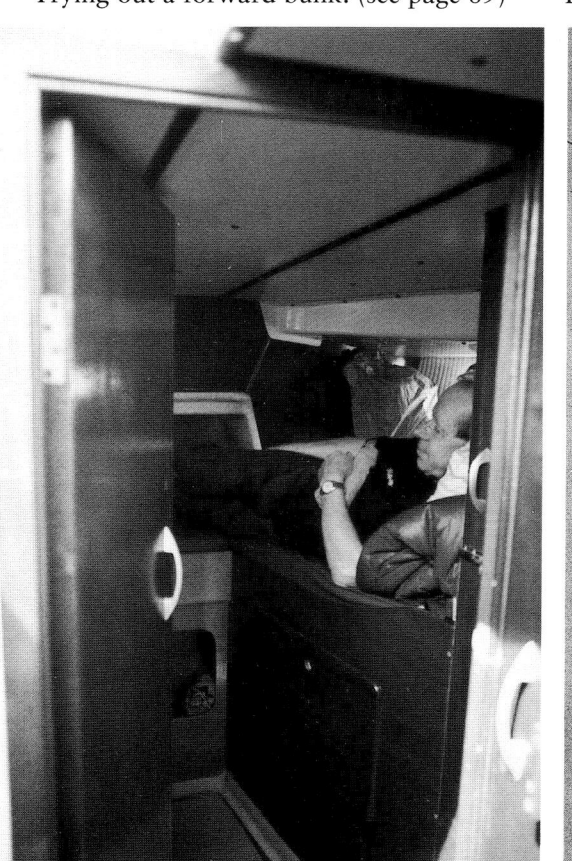

Our landfall. Camp's Bay from Table Mountain.

Left: Journey's end. Alongside at Cape Town.

Below: View to the South Pole: the Cape of Good Hope.

them under his jumper. It wasn't his best joke but it still raised a laugh.

After supper, not knowing what manoeuvring might be needed near harbour, we took in the twin-running sails and carried on under the main and working jib. Shortly after, Bob let the boat gybe badly, the boom swung over with full force and carried away a stopper at the end of a track which held the main-sheet. Fortunately the only damage was that the screw of the stopper sheared off, leaving a bit in the track. We got the sail under control and rigged a rope substitute for the night. The next day Bob fortunately found the stainless-steel stopper and there was enough of the screw left to fix it back in the track again.

From the Swedish ship's information and my noon sight, we expected to sight the Gran Canaria at least before dark. But despite an anxious look-out ahead there was nothing. The hours went by – 2100, 2200, 2300, 2400. By now in the dark we should have been able to pick up La Isleta lighthouse since its visibility was 30 miles. For a daytime landfall there were the 6000 foot mountains of Gran Canaria, but they would have been hidden by cloud.

Still the night wore on and I got more and more worried. After all, we had been 13 days out of sight of land and none of us had had vast experience of ocean navigation. Bob in his bunk was blissfully oblivious, but I kept Jack company and took the helm while he tried to get a radio signal. Unfortunately conditions were bad. With the Sea-Fix kaput, he tried the Sailor radio and got a weak signal, but when he switched to direction-finding it disappeared. The Hitachi was no better. If we were as near as I thought, the signals should have been clear and strong and we wondered if the sets were out of order. At 0200 Jack tried to flash a passing ship but got no reply and she disappeared into the night. I was worried that we might be too far to the east or the west and might have passed, if not the island, then perhaps the light. Gran Canaria is only 20 miles wide and after 13 days at sea our longitude, dependent on time, could possibly be out. And so, through the small hours, we watched and waited in ever greater doubt and anxiety. I think Jack and I affected each other and were more apprehensive together than we would have been alone. At one point we altered course to the east since the lighthouse is more to the east of the island. But since, if there was an error, it was as likely to be one way as the other, we went back to our original course after 20 minutes and stuck to it. Then finally at 0330 we sighted a light dead ahead. By 0400 we could identify the flashes as La Isleta light. Blessed relief! We had made our landfall and except for time, it was spot on.

But what was the reason for the 10 hours delay? I soon found I had made a mistake in correcting the original error in my noon sight. As I said, I had written it as 28° 90′. Then I corrected it to 28° 09′! Idiot! Of course I should have 'carried' 1° and written 29° 30′. It was a difference of 80 miles. But what about the message from the Swedish ship? A hundred miles is a hundred miles. Or is it? I realised that a mile, unlike a kilometre, is not a fixed measure. Even nautical miles differ. There is the Admiralty measured mile of 6080 feet, the English nautical mile of 6082.66 feet, and the International nautical mile (used by the USA) of 6076.1033 feet. If the Swedes had given us land miles there were far larger differences. The original Roman mile was a thousand (mille) double paces or 4833 feet, the statute mile is 5280 feet, the Irish mile 6720 feet, the Scots mile 5928 feet, and the Austrian postal mile 24,000 feet. I believe the Swedes have their own mile and being a big country have made the mile longer to correspond.

9
Las Palmas

At any rate our worries were over. At 0400 Bob came on watch and I turned in. Worn out with a night of nail-biting, I slept until 0500, had a look out to see the light still winking away, seemingly not much nearer, then turned in again and slept until 0800. By then the Gran Canaria, looking dry and treeless, was in full view ahead. Quiet but delighted satisfaction took over. One's first ocean-passage landfall is not just the end of a journey but like being born again.

We got ready to enter harbour, cleared away the anchor – it was stowed on deck – and hoisted our ensign, a courtesy Spanish flag, the yellow Q flag and the Cruising Association burgee. Running under main and jib we gradually passed La Isleta peninsula, a bare, rocky promontory, dominated, it seemed, by the lighthouse and factory sites. Then came the large harbour and the town behind it, houses and high blocks of flats spreading along the shore and up the slopes of the hills. We passed the outer mole called, in the pilot, Digue de Generalissimo Franco. Two large freighters came out of the entrance as we approached and there was movement inside, but there was no entrance control, everything was clear as we came to the end of the breakwater, and we swung round and into the harbour with plenty of room. For the first time in two weeks we were in smooth water.

The quays around, the buildings ahead and the hills behind, were a feast for our eyes, used to looking on the restless sea. I had the added pleasure that we had arrived on my birthday and without advertising the fact, could enjoy the town, the fresh food and a full eight hours sleep as a celebration. There was a busy traffic of small craft coming and going – launches, small freighters, tenders, tugs – and the quays were lined with passenger and cargo boats. We crossed an outer harbour in one tack and after passing another sea wall, could see on the far side a cluster of masts. The yachts were grouped at anchor, and there was room for us to come into a vacant space under sail, and let go the anchor. The water was clear and it seemed a good anchorage, but we were not to stay free of oil for long. It was 1130 as we hauled the sails down.

Almost at once we had a visit from a girl in a dinghy, who came neatly alongside, shipped her oars and introduced herself as Sue. We met two couples from yachts nearby, both friendly and helpful – Sue and Chris, Agnetta and Pepe. Sue and Chris had a smartish production boat, a 27-foot sloop. They had made their way from England via Vigo, Portugal and Madeira. They had left from the South Coast in April and taken their time. The highlight had been a call at Selvagem Island lying halfway between Madeira and the Canaries, where they had spent over a week. They found a sheltered anchorage but would have had to move with a change of wind. The place was completely deserted. There were plenty of fish in the sea, rabbits and pigeons ashore, and they lived off the land. There was only one house on the island, occupied, they said, for part of the year by an English naturalist, who was put ashore and picked up again by a Spanish fishing boat. They hated to leave such an idyllic spot but they were running short of some supplies. One wonders there should be an uninhabited island so near civilisation, and perhaps Selvagem has not remained such a Garden of Eden.

Agnetta and Pepe had come from Spain. Agnetta was Swedish and had been on a working holiday when they met. Pepe had got tired of working in his father's construction business in Castellon, a town on the coast south of Barcelona, and they had acquired their rather battered old yacht and set off without any cut-and-dried plan. They had made their way via Gibraltar, down the African coast and across to Fuerteventura. There they had had a bad storm and just managed to make port safely at night. Both couples seemed well settled in Las Palmas, knew the local markets and shops, and offered to help us buy supplies or get repairs done. The local yacht club, they said, was not very welcoming and though visiting yachtsmen could have showers and use changing rooms they were not allowed in the rest of the premises.

In the afternoon we rowed ashore and asked at the yacht club for a mechanic who could look at the engine, but without success. Language was a difficulty and Pepe's help, especially with the centreboard, was invaluable. From the club I went to the central Post Office, but arrived too late and found it closed. Taking a tram back north along the main street (trams were cheap and frequent) to another club, the Club Moto-Nautico, I again asked for a mechanic for marine engines, but again without success. Before I went back to the boat I was able to change some money in a hotel and buy some postcards.

The next morning I went ashore with Agnetta who was going shopping in the market and would show me where it was. It was not far from the yacht club, two blocks off the main road, a large two-storey building packed with stalls on the ground floor and tucked away upstairs, as Agnetta explained in attractive broken English, were the lower-priced wholesale lots sold by the case, or the hundred (oranges), and also bargain lots of damaged or over-ripe fruit and vegetables. I had a good look round partly for the pleasure of looking, partly for future reference when we would all three come and stock up for the next leg. There were plenty of potatoes, pumpkins, prickly pear, avocados, tomatoes, melons, pomegranates, custard apples; bloody-looking meat stalls; fish of all kinds, squid, espadon (swordfish), oysters, clams and other shell fish.

I left Agnetta shopping and went on by tram into town. I had the Sea-Fix with the broken switch ready packed and at the Post Office was able to send it to the makers in Poole for about £1.50. I asked them to repair it and send it *post restante* to Cape Town and my bank would meet the cost of repair. I wrote to the bank at the same time. There were a few letters waiting for us and I sent some personal mail. One reason I had bought the Sailor radio was because the Danish makers offered world-wide service. But when I called at the address in the list – *Refa. Etel (Sr Suarez o Sr Quevado) Calle Leon y Castillo 141 Las Palmas* – they had moved and nobody knew where. But the man next door spoke English, was helpful and rang Hispano Radio Maritime, who promised to come down to *Swingaway* at 3 pm. While I was doing this, Bob had been out with Pepe by car to a factory in the country and got two containers of gas. Jack had been busy on board fitting corks round the shrouds where the mainsail, used so much for running, had begun to show black marks, and where we feared it might start to wear. Come 3 pm there was no sign of Hispano Radio, but a sailmaker came out and collected the sails for overhaul and repair. Pepe promised to take me to the welder for the centre-board casting on Wednesday morning. That evening for supper we had pork chops fried in breadcrumbs, vin rosé, parmesan cheese and figs.

Wednesday morning Pepe collected me with the broken part of the centre-board and we went to the welding shop. Unfortunately the boss, Mario, wasn't there and nothing could be done. A friend of Pepe's rang another radio firm, Nautico, who also promised to come at 3 pm. At the *poste restante* I got a letter for Jack. Back at the yacht Jack and Bob had drained the petrol tank until not a drop of water remained and put in new plugs, but the engine was missing as badly as ever. For lunch we had grapes and tomatoes and tasty Spanish *chorizos* (a kind of sausage). At 3 pm the Nautico radio men arrived, tried out the Sailor, said it was fine and went off without charging. At 4 pm three couples invited by Bob arrived for tea. At the same time, a day late, Hispano Radio turned up in a rakish launch, looked at the Sailor, pronounced it in perfect order, and roared away also without charging. After tea Pepe and I went back to the welding shop but Mario was again missing.

I was concerned about the engine and went on a wild goose chase to the north of the town and the head of the harbour where everyone said I was sure to find a) a mechanic, and b) a boat-hook. I also wanted some methylated spirits for starting the Tilley lamp and some turps substitute or white spirit for painting jobs. I was looking for two signs – *Talleres Navales* or Marine Engineers and *Effectos Navales* or Ship Chandlers. As I walked along the character of the streets changed. They were older and there were more repair yards. I passed the landmark I had been given, *el Castillo*, an old fort. Here was where the big ships docked and were repaired. After enquiring, I found my way to two *Talleres*, but neither would help. One shop (they were working on a huge propeller shaft) said they couldn't do anything under two months. The other sounded interested until I said it was a petrol engine – they only repaired diesels.

I found my way to a large, crowded *Effectos Navales* where they were selling quantities of rope and paint and rigging-wire and blocks, and had sextants and compasses under glass. My Spanish is rudimentary and the phrase-book I had was better at phrases like 'What is the price for each piece of luggage?' or 'We want to take a coach tour round the sights' than 'Have you got a boat-hook – or turps substitute – or meths?' Holding a conversation was like being in a mist where you couldn't see where you were going, or see other people coming. For you could neither express yourself clearly nor understand the reply. However, they were very amiable and I was taken behind the counter and shown all their stock on endless shelves. I soon found some turpentine, the real thing from a turpentine tree. I had not seen real turpentine for years and the tree-y, resinous scent of it brought back childhood memories of white-coated painters mixing their colours like artists. Methylated spirits (I tried the French *alcool à brûler*) they didn't seem to have.

Nor despite their large stock did they have a boat-hook. They understood what I wanted and discussed my drawing calling it 'bichero' and shaking their heads. I might have got a kind of hook as a substitute, but there was a hullabaloo at the door, all business came to an end, and the shop-assistants rushed out to see. It was a mini-accident. An old man in a wheel-chair had been run into by a moped. He wasn't hurt, just very indignant, waving his stick and scolding the moped rider. The young cyclist, on the defensive, tried to excuse himself, pick up his moped and brush his clothes, all at the same time. I gave up and left.

On the way back to *Swingaway* I saw a large *Effectos Navales* painted on a wall and walked in. It turned out I had come into the back of the shop and there I was, in the back parlour, in among the family, mother, children, the cat. I was halfway through the room before I realized it, but none of them stopped me, took any notice of me, or even interrupted their conversation. So I walked through to the shop beyond where an assistant explained it was shut, *cerrado*, and let me out the front way. I got back to the yacht anchorage depressed, and it was no consolation that I couldn't attract anybody's attention from the shore and had to wait half-an-hour and beg a lift out to *Swingaway* in another dinghy. I had hardly got anything we needed. No mechanic, no boat-hook. We had not even delivered the broken centre-board fitting. I remembered other fruitless expeditions on foot through other foreign ports, baffled by the language barrier, by inevitable delays, by the traveller's ignorance and helplessness.

On the brighter side Bob seemed happier about the engine and we had another good meal, this time of fresh fish, white wine and a delicious melon. Also a most surprising thing had happened – there was another Ocean Bird in harbour! Jack had been across to see and there were two men on board. They were to come and pay us a visit the next evening. Charlie Hughes was the owner and he had come out from Dartmouth with Peter his cousin. They had set out the same time as we had, but had had a slower passage. Charlie had done some single-handed cruises, and told us a hair-raising story of breaking his rudder when a hundred miles off one of the West Indies. For three days he worked on his own trying to rig up a makeshift rudder from one of the cupboard doors. Heaving up and down at the stern in a rubber dinghy, it was slow and disheartening work.

On one occasion all the tools in the dinghy went overboard. He managed finally to rig up a jury rudder and limp to the nearest port. After that, like us, he carried a spare rudder. This was the second rudder failure I had heard about.

All the same he was sold on his Ocean Bird and he was planning an indefinite cruise, again to the West Indies, through the Canal and on to the South Seas. He was going to stay several months in the Canaries and have self-steering fitted, probably an Aries. On reflection it was surprising that, as a single-hander, he hadn't already a 100 per cent system. We exchanged notes about a lot of points and he admired the interior of *Swingaway*, which was better fitted than his boat. What he said about the floats on his boat gave me cause for a lot of thought. When he drained them he got 27 gallons of water from each float. *Swingaway*'s floats had yielded only a gallon each, which agreed with John Westell's estimate. Whether Charlie had another kind of foam perhaps, or whether there was a lot of water in *Swingaway*'s floats that hadn't drained out, there seemed no means of telling. At any rate Charlie had had inspection hatches put in which enabled him to pump the floats out whenever he liked. I decided to do something if I could at Cape Town, but events made it unnecessary.

Thursday was sunny, the barometer showed 1028 millibars and the wind backed for an hour to blow from the west instead of the prevailing north-east. The water had been clean when we came in, but successive oil patches had made the topsides filthy, and as a trimaran we had that much more waterline. Choosing a time when there was no oil I managed to have a bathe and washed the floats and main hull with petrol. But my cleaning brought more oil, and soon everything was as black as before. I repainted the name on each float since two weeks at sea had washed away parts of some of the letters. The engine, praise be, was going well at last. In our last effort, going beyond the directions in the instruction book, we had taken the carburettor down more fully than before and found drops of water in a minute chamber. So we had fixed it ourselves. Triumph!

Pepe and I went a third time to the welding yard. At last we met the elusive Mario, who agreed to do the work by Friday afternoon for about 600 pesetas. On Friday it was ready as promised and a good strong job, though the cost came to 950 pesetas instead of 600. Still it didn't seem too much at about £7. When we fitted it, it worked, and we had the satisfaction of winding the centre-board up and down under complete control.

We spent most of Friday morning in the market where we laid out £10 on eggs, fruit, vegetables, meat, bread, wine and beer. We concentrated on fresh food which was cheap and good. Tinned food cost more than in England and in any case we had plenty on board. Butter and cheese were dear. We already had a good stock of margarine which had kept well. The sailmaker brought the sails back and charged only a few pounds for his work. After we got back from market I found that a book of traveller's cheques I had been carrying in the hip-pocket of my jeans, was gone. The pocket was fairly shallow, and it had most likely fallen out. Nowadays one would be certain that it was the work of a pickpocket. I wrote to the bank then and there asking them to cancel all except the two cheques I had already cashed, and asked them to send an equivalent amount (£250) to the bank in Cape Town.

That night Agnetta and Pepe, and Sue and Chris, came for supper. Bob gave us an enormous meal of tomato salad, chicken Maryland and pancakes. He and Jack went on producing one lot of pancakes after another until none of us could eat any more. I remember drinking a good deal (no driving to worry about) and have a vague recollection of warm farewells after midnight and the guests rowing unsteadily back to their yachts. Our plan was to leave the next day.

10

SECOND WIND

On Saturday morning we filled the water-tanks and all our containers. Even if we had taken *Swingaway* alongside, there was no water piped to the yacht-club jetty, so we had to bring it all out in the dinghy. Jack finished putting corks on the shrouds. We got the dinghy stowed away on deck, sails bent on, and everything ready to weigh anchor. In the end Las Palmas had been good to us. We had got everything checked or repaired at modest cost. We had all had a thorough rest with five full nights in our bunks. We had feasted on fresh food for five days and had a lot of enjoyable yarning with fellow yachtsmen. Even if we had spent time fruitlessly in the dusty streets, and if we hadn't had leisure to explore the interior – these were minor drawbacks.

We weighed anchor after lunch at 1330 and left under the engine, waving as we passed Pepe's boat with his dog barking farewell, and then Charlie Hughes's Ocean Bird. In the outer harbour we hoisted the main and the genoa, and with the wind abeam on the port tack we ran out and then down the coast on a course of 170°. At 1405, a mile from the entrance, we streamed the log. By 1900 we were round Point Tenefe towards the south of the island and, on a course of 230° with a light following breeze, hoisted the twin-running rig. We passed the airport with a succession of planes turning into the wind to land, and others taking off. By 2130 there were 23 miles on the log, and as the sun left the sky the bare hills took on beautiful grey shades. On our starboard beam the Morro de Colchas light began winking away. It seemed we had said goodbye to the Canaries.

But we hadn't. The breeze died away completely and we lay there all night. The log-line went down vertically into the sea and before we could take it in, got tangled round the rudder and propeller. With one of us working in the water which was hardly cold, and another shining a torch over the stern, we got it clear. By morning there was still land mistily visible to the north. At 0900 a light breeze sprang up from the south-west and we began to make 1 or 2 knots on a course of 200°. At this rate it would take us six months to get to Cape Town. Then the wind died again completely. We swam and cleaned the boat of some of the harbour oil. By noon we had only 30 miles on the log. The meridian altitude gave us 27° 29' north. There was a light breeze at lunch then again dead calm. We swam, and lay on our bunks, slept and read.

I got on into my two books of crossword puzzles from the *Telegraph* and the *Guardian*. I was also gradually reading Shakespeare, the plays I'd always missed seeing or reading, mostly the lesser known ones: *Measure for Measure, Titus Andronicus, Troilus and Cressida, Timon of Athens, Cymbeline, Pericles Prince of Tyre, Two Gentlemen of Verona, The Comedy of Errors, Much Ado about Nothing, Love's Labour Lost* – the list went on and on. I had enough reading for weeks. Bob shared the book and, following an entirely different plan, he read through the historical plays. He started at *King John* and *Richard the Second* but whether he got to *Henry the Eighth* I am not sure. Jack read about King Arthur and Tintagel. He was also studying maths and got lessons from Bob who had a maths degree and had been teaching the subject. They used to mull over algebra and trigonometry and Jack kept saying: 'I'm not very good at maths. That's why I want to learn it.'

All afternoon there were porpoises plunging round the boat. We had seen a few north of the Canaries but from now on they were to become more common. On this occasion they were the smaller porpoises and we more often saw schools of dolphins. Both species are kinds of small whales, to the untrained observer not very different from one another. Porpoises are bluer, dolphins more brown or grey. Porpoises are smaller and chubbier, dolphins larger with a beak-like snout. Both swim round boats; it is the dolphins who more deliberately 'play' with them.

They seemed to enjoy it most when we were going at a good lick, at six or seven knots. They would swim in from the side, fast shadows moving just under the surface, then swish past the bow, missing it by a hairbreadth. Then they would come in again – and again – and again. Sometimes they would vary the angle. Sometimes they would come in pairs, in threes, up to six at a time. They were like rugger players, dodging, interweaving – untouchable, uncatchable. Apparently they navigate by sound or ultrasonic pulses, which would explain their ability to flash past the boat and one another. They could hardly do it by eyesight. When they had been diving round the boat for a long time I would get obsessed with the feeling that they would make a slip and damage the hull. But they never did. They were there at night too. Like phosphorescent torpedoes they put on their own marine firework display.

Day after day we lived on, in, near the sea, almost part of it. Passengers on a great cruise liner are remote from any water but the swimming-pool – that is except for distant views and hypnotised contemplation of the boiling wake. To see the full wonder of this other universe you have to take a face-mask, a pair of flippers and a snorkel, or a lung, and dive, as I have done, in teeming tropical waters. But a small yacht gets you close – dolphin, porpoise, flying-fish, phosphorescent plancton, and bathing a thousand miles from shore in a pool 4000 fathoms deep. And the never-ending motion, the sound and smells and excitement of the sea itself, are more powerful and yet more peaceful.

A light wind, enough for 2 knots, came that night from the south-east, then in the morning watch it veered to west-south-west. The third day at sea we passed a P-and-O boat. The barometer stood at 1024 millibars, my watch was 31 seconds slow on GMT and a morning sight (azimuth 94°) gave us 16° 30′ west. For plotting sights I began to use the plotting sheets we had bought and found them useful. The Atlantic Ocean chart was on too small a scale to plot an intercept, and these sheets had the same proportions as Mercator charts. As we were travelling from north to south, we covered a wide range of latitudes, and as each plotting sheet covered only 3° of latitude or 180 miles I got through them quite quickly. Also there were several sheets missing when I had been in the shop – 18° to 21° and 30° to 39°. Bob, being a mathematician, was by now as expert at navigation as I was, and he had a shot at making substitutes on the back of a chart, but it was tedious and tricky work. The day's noon sight put us 26° 45′ north and we got an RDF bearing on Villa Cisneros of 180°. On the log there were only 75 miles. Seventy-five miles in three days. It was disheartening.

Being becalmed at sea is in its way as bad as any other hazards. Storms? Yes – damaging, terrifying, dangerous. But at least *something is happening*. If you drop a matchstick over the side at night and it's still there in the morning . . . and the next morning . . . and the next . . . Then a sort of heart-sickness begins to affect you. If your car breaks down or you wait an hour for a bus, at least you can walk. Perhaps I'm impatient. But I still remember with dread three days becalmed in the Mediterranean, and though we didn't have anything as bad on this voyage, you couldn't say we made a fast passage.

However, we washed clothes in the morning and ran the engine and it still seemed OK. Then in the afternoon the wind freshened and soon backed to the north. At last after three days of calms we seemed to be back to trade winds. We changed the mainsail and jib for the twin-running sails just before dark, and carried them through the night. For lunch we had salad and sardines, for supper ham, potatoes and tinned vegetables. By the morning of the fourth day the log showed 168 miles and at noon 182.

Just after lunch we were overtaken by a French destroyer, the *Argenais*. She came very near and when we gave them a hail the sailors on deck waved back. As we usually did when a ship was near we hoisted our ensign. Our torch being far too weak for daytime signalling, this time Jack decided to try semaphore. The British calling-up sign in semaphore is to move the arms up-and-down from a position by the sides to a horizontal position. It so happens there is a distress signal, a visual SOS, made by moving the arms up-and-down from a position by the sides to vertically over the head. I am pretty sure the Frenchmen mistook Jack's waving for an SOS. For instead of replying in French semaphor (I doubt if we could have read it), the destroyer came to a stop two or three cables away and began to lower a rubber rescue-boat. Very likely it was also in the nature of an exercise. We took our sails down when we saw what they were up to, and like Dignity and Impudence we lay together in the light swell. To the uninvolved observer (God?) it must have looked hilarious.

There were as I remember, four men and an officer in the rubber boat driven by a heavy outboard. They came up alongside the counter and when I invited them aboard for a drink in my best French, the officer seemed to ignore my invitation and asked in English: 'Do-you-want-anything?' First we asked him to report us to Lloyds of London. He got out his radio telephone and with some repetition of the name *Swing-a-way* passed our request back. Then we asked him for our position as a check and again after some delay he gave us the information. The position we got from them was 25° 23.2' north 17° 34' west. Our own reckoning at midday was 25° 23' north 27° 31' west. So with all the trials and errors of taking sights in a bouncing yacht, with our cheap plastic sextant and a wristwatch for chronometer – there was less than a mile difference in latitude and only 3 miles difference in longitude. My confidence in my navigation was much increased – and so I expect was Bob's and Jack's!

The *Argenais*, they told us, was bound for Dakar and they expected to get there the next day, 12 September. Our French visitors wouldn't come on board for a drink, so after we had shaken hands with the officer and thanked him as best we could, they motored off. We got the twin-running sails up again and on our course of 220°. We had been stopped I suppose about an hour, and the visit helped to make up for the three days' slow progress, which had rather got us down. Also they did in fact report us to Lloyds, the only ship which did, though Jack thought he had made contact with two other ships at least. If our cruise had been three months later we might have done better with the flag hoist 'Z D 2' – 'Please report me to Lloyds London' – which came into use in January of the following year. Also, when we had seen the French destroyer slowing down, Jack had tried to make contact with our Safety Link, the emergency battery-powered telephone transmitter tuned permanently to the distress frequency, 2182 Kc. But he got no reply. It all goes to show the difficulty of communications at sea for a small boat.

The fifth day out from Las Palmas the following wind continued stronger with a heavier swell. We ran on under the twin sails still enjoying the benefit of self-steering with the sheets led to the tiller. Now there was sun every day, blue water, and we were travelling continually through shoals of flying-fish. Hour after hour we rushed on doing a steady 6 knots or better. Now we were making good progress with over 300 miles on the log. We had been in the water a lot since Las Palmas but now leisurely swimming was out of the question, though we managed to get a shower bath by sitting or lying on one of the floats. Then that evening came the first of a series of troubles with the forward halyards.

For the twin-running sails we had been using the jib halyard and the spinnaker halyard, both with ends forward of the mast. With the main halyard aft of the mast, these were the only three halyards fitted at the mast head. For another long ocean passage, I would like to have at least one, or better two, extra halyards ready rove. We were trying to adjust the twin rig to alter course from 220° to 215° when the wire jib halyard, which held the port running-sail, broke and the sail came tumbling down and was flogging furiously. At the same time, in the panic, one of us let the sheet of the starboard sail slip from its cleat. To get the sail at right angles to the wind on the new course, the pole had been brought aft of a starboard shroud. So when the sheet slipped, the metal pole, a tube with no lateral strength, was bent at a right angle. There we were with a broken halyard and a broken spinnaker-pole. Repairs had to wait until morning. For the night we took the good pole over to the starboard side and carried on under a single starboard running sail. We were back to continuous heavy steering, and the wind had got up so much we were doing 5 to 6 knots under one sail.

We could see from the running sail still set why the halyard had broken. The head of the sail was bobbing about continuously in the wind, and the spinnaker halyard that had survived was rope and evidently less likely to fray with movement of this kind than wire. Even so spinnakers are intended to be carried for a few hours in a race, or a day or two at most, not for weeks on end. We had had the twin-running rig set for ten days in all. The halyard block on *Swingaway* was rigid on the mast and referring back to the original twin-running design, which I had copied, I found the halyard was shown going through a block hung from a strop round the mast so that it could follow the movement of the sail in the wind. On *Swingaway* as an alternative I could have fixed the sails on a stay, which would have held the head steady like the head of a jib.

We had spare rigging wire but it would be easier to repair the broken halyard than cut a new one. Even that meant a wire splice in stainless steel and re-reeving it at the mast head. Jack, an expert at rope work including wire, set to work with a will, but without proper tools it took him two days to produce even a rough result. In any case there was too much sea for climbing the mast to be comfortable and we couldn't very well use the twin sails until they had been modified. In the meantime we set the big genoa on the starboard side (we were steering 210° with the wind on the port quarter) and the storm jib on the port side on the main halyard. We were making good speed and *Swingaway* seemed comfortable.

Bob took charge of mending the broken spinnaker-pole and when it came to emergency repairs he was full of ingenuity. In this case we straightened out the pole and put wood splints along the side, jammed into place by driving them through empty food-tins. With top and bottom removed these formed metal bands which held the splints in place. We tested it by booming out a sail and it stood up all right in the strong wind. The greatest drawback in losing the twin rig was having no means of self-steering so long as the wind was astern. We tried a system using the storm-jib backed to windward forward of the mast, but it was no good with the wind astern or on the quarter.

In these days as we were rounding the bulge of Africa, we got some radio bearings as a check on our sun sights. The third day out, Jack got Monrovia but only a vague direction since it had no beacon. The same day we got the bearing already mentioned on Villa Cisneros and we were to pick it up on three subsequent days with the bearing changing from 180° to 85°. The sixth day we picked up Sal in the Cape Verde Islands bearing (doubtfully) 210°, and on subsequent days it altered to 230°, 243°, and 324°. Signals from Sal were strong but with much interference. From the Cape Verde Islands on, we could get no signals from the radio beacons at Dakar or Sierra Leone, presumably because we were too far out to sea. Later in the voyage on the twenty-eighth day from Las Palmas in 10° south, we picked up Ascension Island and Recife in Brazil. The Ascension signal was strong enough to get a bearing vaguely to the east. Recife was just audible on the main Sailor set but not at all on the direction-finder.

As we relied more and more on sun sights, the main use of the radio was to get time signals. We found the clearest were the BBC short-wave transmissions beamed to Africa and (later) South America, and got sometimes the 8 o'clock and sometimes the 9 o'clock time signal. The signals came about breakfast time since our ship's time was approximately the same as BST. We also listened to the news and bits of other programmes. The Overseas Service exports the British way of life, including a cosy friendliness, and we would hear the disc jockey announcing: 'Good morning Mrs Owololo of Umbunga. Many happy returns. Here is your birthday request, "Knock, knock, knock" played by the Low Down Swingers.'

The reception was not good enough for music and there wasn't anything on the Overseas Service like the continuous flow of the Third Programme. This was a real loss. Perhaps I had thought too exclusively about sailing and safety, food and drink. Perhaps I had thought radio reception would be better. Books, games and crosswords are OK, but anyone who loves music should take some tapes and a player. There was one advantage. When I did get back to listening again, the magic of Mozart came through new ears. Ears starved for three months. I still remember that first delight and I expect one can indulge in over-listening just as in over-eating. At any rate starvation improves the appetite.

11
Cape Verde and Beyond

With all the flying fish round the boat some began to land on board. The day after we met the destroyer we picked one up on deck and had fish for tea. That night on watch, I heard a thump and a skittering sound, and there was another in the scuppers. By morning we had several more so we had fried flying fish for breakfast. Every morning after that I went round the deck to see what I could find, since they came on board more during the night. One day there were more than six flying fish plus a small squid. Jack and Bob both went off them after a while, but I never got sick of them. I would have my flying fish for breakfast while they shared a tin of beans. They were like fresh herring, small fish with a lot of fine bones, and perhaps the other two got tired of trying to negotiate the bones. Perhaps the most delicious were the tiny ones the size of a finger, fried and eaten whole like whitebait.

During the day they flew away from the boat, spraying out from the bow and travelling an amazing distance through the air. They seemed to go farther when the sea was lumpy and often it was hard to see where they flopped into the water again. Sometimes they would 'skip' on the water several times before they submerged. They glide rather than fly and the species we saw (there are forty) had the forward fins enlarged to gliding wings. It must be a good means of escape. What could baffle a big fish more than to have its prey literally disappear into thin air? From 15° north to 15° south the shoals were large and the fish themselves small. As we got farther south perhaps the species changed, for the individual fish were larger but the shoals less frequent and smaller. At 28° to 30° south, they thinned out and disappeared.

Our course south was determined by two guides. *Ocean Passages for the World* published in 1923, was a work with excellent maps giving directions for sailing ships on ocean voyages in every part of the globe. I had consulted it in the Cruising Association and copied out the relevant parts for England to Cape Town and across the Indian Ocean. Our second guide was a Routeing Chart for the South Atlantic for the month of September. We didn't reach the Southern Hemisphere until the end of September, but we assumed average winds would not be too different, and pored over the chart and discussed how far south and how far east we should go.

The advice on *Ocean Passages* was good on the whole. The first point was to make a good Westing before crossing the Bay of Biscay. A second passage advised passing to the west of the Cape Verde Islands where there was likely to be more wind. Because we had called at Las Palmas the course to the east of the islands was the more direct, but sure enough we were to be becalmed for almost a day in sight of land. For crossing the Line and the passage south the advice was as follows: 'In July, August and September the southerly winds will be met with between 10° and 12° north latitudes. On meeting them steer on the starboard tack to cross the 5° parallel between 17° and 19° west. Then steer on the other tack to cross the Equator between 25° and 23° west longitude.' (For October, November and December the recommendation was to cross 5° north between 23° and 25° west and the Equator between 24° and 29° west).

'Having crossed the Equator stand across the south-east Trade wind on the port tack even should the vessel fall off to the west by south for the wind will draw more to the eastward as the vessel advances and finally to the east at the southern limit of the Trades. When to the south of the south-east Trades the vessel will generally meet fresh winds variable in direction. From Trinidad [this is not Trinidad in the West Indies but a smaller island 20° south] a course should be shaped to the south eastward to cross the parallel of 30° south in about longitude 22° west and the meridian of Greenwich in about 35° to 37° south. Whence to the Cape of Good Hope winds from the westward and southward usually prevail.'

In a modern yacht with a Bermuda rig sailing closer to the wind, it is not necessary as we found, to make such a long detour at the southern limit of the Trades. But for the rest we generally followed the book. Thus our plan was to cross the Equator in longitude 20° to 27° west, then to skirt the edge of the Trades quite near South America, gradually curving in east towards Cape Town, approaching it from the west. There were no dangers though I worried about St Paul Rocks in 1° north, 29° west, mainly perhaps because they were off the edge of our chart (we had only the *South Atlantic – Ocean Eastern Portion*) and hence invisible.

The seventh day from Las Palmas, a day after breaking the halyard, the wind fell and veered to the east. We hoisted the main and ran on the port tack with both the main and genoa on the starboard side. I lost our only bucket overboard, letting go of the rope as I pitched it over to get water for washing the deck. We made up something from a food tin but it was a poor substitute and I missed it for the rest of the voyage. Since we had two of almost everything, it was foolish not to have carried a second bucket.

The day before there had been a shark circling the boat, its sharp fin as ominous as a periscope in wartime. This day we saw a school of whales but at a good distance. Bob and Jack made some makeshift spinners to use with our fish-hooks, hoping we might catch something bigger than the flying fish. Over quite some time, they tried all sorts of bait and sizes of hook, but didn't manage to catch a single fish. We were really going too fast for serious fishing, and I think on the whole coastal shelves are richer. After all, we were in thousands of fathoms.

The eighth day there were 690 miles on the log, my watch was 65 seconds slow on GMT and the sun sights put us 21° 55′ west 17° 40′ north. I was lucky to get a morning sight as there was nearly 95 per cent cloud and we had a shower of rain at 0800. It was the morning sun that was more likely to be obscured. The noonday sun seemed to disperse the clouds or shine through them and there were only a few days on the whole voyage when it was totally invisible at noon.

That afternoon the wind veered more to the south until for a while we were on an easy beat. Under these conditions the stay-sail forward of the mast with sheet led to the tiller worked well as an automatic helmsman. The weather was changing from the freshness of the Canaries, getting hotter and hotter. At night in the cabin it was too warm to sleep well. The Walker log began to give trouble. It was not turning freely and under-reading as a result. If I oiled it well it would be all right for a time and then get stiff again. It evidently needed expert attention. We still had the electric log which seemed reliable.

The ninth day we sighted land at 1130. The wind was down to Force 3 and all that afternoon we lay becalmed, rolling about in a moderate swell and in sweltering heat, off Boa Vista, a blue shape seen hazily some 10 to 20 miles away. That was all we saw of the

Cape Verde Islands. Sal, Santiago and Maio were too far to the west to be visible. Gradually at the end of the day the wind increased, this time from the north-west, and we ran on towards our next objective, the Equator, steering 205° and again on the starboard tack. Again we were up to 5 or 6 knots with 790 miles on the log. We saw no lighthouse on the Island, presumably being too far south. In the early morning a cargo ship had passed us going north and we saw the lights of another northbound ship in the evening.

During the day Bob and I mended the WC, a tedious job that meant screwing and unscrewing bolts in the most awkward positions. It was not pumping water in from the sea and we found that the rubber diaphragm of the main pump had split. We had a kit of various spare parts and were able to put in a new diaphragm. Earlier on, because of other breakdowns, we had put up a notice for the benefit of all three of us. It read:

PLEASE

1. Flush out with sea water after use (handle inward).
2. Wipe bowl if necessary with paper or brush.
3. Use light at night.
4. Treat pump gently.

(SANITATION DEPARTMENT NOTICE)

I also took advantage of the calm to go up to the top of the mast and re-reeve the jib halyard that Jack had spliced. It was a good thing I did, because the next day Jack showed me the spinnaker halyard.

'Look at that,' he said, 'the rats have been at it.'

Jack was supreme head of this department and he took pride in it. I even felt (perhaps with a grain of irritation) that he wasn't displeased when something went wrong, as it gave him a chance to exercise his skills, and make his specialist contribution in this field, as opposed to fixing the engine or navigating. The halyard had lasted better than the wire but it was badly frayed and it wouldn't be long before it went. We decided to turn it end for end, Jack got on with the splicing straight away, and as it was an easier job, completed it the same day.

With the wind dead aft and the jib not setting properly on either side, we had been running under main alone. After dark it was more on the beam, but when we tried to hoist the jib we could hardly pull it up. There was so much resistance we decided to leave it until morning. The next morning at 0600 the wind drew ahead and *Swingaway* refused to hold her course without a head sail. At 0700 we tried to hoist the jib again and found the same resistance. Though the sea was rough I decided to go up, take the respliced halyard and have a look at the jib-halyard block. It meant lowering the mainsail and going up on the main halyard, the only one of the three still functioning. At the top I was swinging with the mast in an arc of three or four feet, and had to cling like a leech. But I was able to reeve the spinnaker halyard. I found that the pulley-wheel in the jib-halyard block (which fitted close between the top of the mast and the forestay) was somehow jammed. I tried to turn it with my fingers but it was immovable. It explained why we were having difficulty, but there was nothing I could do to fix it. However, knowing what was wrong, we were able to go on using the block by taking things gently, easing the sail up, and gradually dragging the wire through the pulley and over the sheave. By 0900 we were under way, beating into the wind a few points free.

A few days after this one or two of the corks on the lower shrouds started to come loose, and threatened to go overboard if not attended to. There was little wind and it seemed a good time to go up, this time only to the cross trees. I was getting ready to get into our bosun's chair (a wooden board on rope, like a swing seat) when Jack volunteered to go up instead. Both Bob and I had been up the mast at sea and Jack had been up and put the corks on in harbour. True to our agreement that everyone should have a go at everything I told him to go ahead. When one of us was up the mast, the other two stood below, hauling the chair up, sending up any extra tools needed. Jack started off all right but then he seemed to get agitated at any delay. We were doing things as quickly as we could, but we had to be careful especially on the cabin top and twice had to go and get things – some more tape and a piece of wire. When Jack came down he was beside himself and stormed at two rather astonished people – 'When I give you orders you bloody well jump to it.' However, he simmered down quickly and took it without a murmur when I told him it wasn't a question of him giving orders and he was not to go up the mast again. Bob or I would do it. In a short time we were all having a drink together.

The illustration of one of the fo'c'sle bunks (plate 4) looks pretty claustrophobic. Of course the main cabin was bigger and the bunk folded to make a couch during the day. Then again we spent time on deck or in the large cockpit. Even so anybody might think that three men in a small boat for nearly three months would generate explosive antagonisms. But it wasn't like that. What I've described was one of only two or three incidents. On the whole, considering everything, we kept on very good terms. Jack was temperamental sometimes as the cruise went on. On a later occasion he was clearly very depressed and didn't speak to us for two days, and missed a couple of meals. He had sudden enthusiasms, would stay up to take star sights, make elaborate dishes, sweets and puddings. At other times he would be late on watch or shirk his share of the chores. Once he told us bluntly, 'I intend to look after myself.'

'You mean pull the ladder up Jack, I'm all right?' I suggested.

'No. I don't mean that.'

And he didn't. He was reacting, I think, to a lonely childhood and having been shoved into the Navy at the age of thirteen or fourteen. No doubt he had had to look after himself. If sometimes unpredictably prickly, at other times he had sudden generous impulses, would give away his share of food, or do extra work to relieve somebody else.

Jack had a fascinating fund of information about warships and navies, foreign as well as British. Like others I've known who have lived on the lower deck, he was a great raconteur. Perhaps his best story was about a message in a bottle. One of the sailors on HMS *Zulu*, as a joke, when they were on exercises in the North Sea, wrote out a message, 'I AM BEING HELD PRISONER ON HMS ZULU. COME TO THE RESCUE, Signed – Billy Binns.' He put it in a bottle and threw it overboard. By an extraordinary chance the bottle was washed ashore and picked up unbroken. The person who picked it up for whatever reason, sent the message to the Admiralty. Slowly but surely the message found its way back to HMS *Zulu* and Seaman W. Binns (for he had lightheartedly signed his own name) was asked to explain . . .

Although it was my boat and I had organised the cruise, I tried not to think of myself as 'Skipper' or to come the heavy. The need for this depends on the situation: three people with the same interest and object (getting there) is a very different matter from a crew of 300 with possibly divergent or conflicting interests. Perhaps I was too easy. As I explain later, an accident to the main boom was caused because I avoided confronting Jack. He wanted to do one thing, I wanted to do the other. I wasn't certain, I hesitated and didn't insist, but as it turned out he was wrong. On the other hand when we had a more serious accident to the rudder, Jack's determination and energy was a vital factor in coping with the damage.

Bob was completely different. Big, good natured, easy going, he had been brought up in a large family, been good both at games and work and turned his hand to various jobs both academic and practical, all the more varied since he had been knocking round the world. He enjoyed company and was great with kids as I found later in Cape Town. Within minutes he had them rapt with attention and eating out of his hand. He had a flair, perhaps from his teaching, for putting things simply and bringing them alive. On the voyage he was always doing more than his share and would turn his hand to anything. Though we all took turns, he was the best cook and organised any parties we had in harbour. Half way through the voyage he knew as much about navigation as I did, though he was content to leave the routine to me. He was strong as a horse, yet when the compass light failed he handled its thread-like wires with the lightest fingers.

I had my moments, but I had fits of depression too. For instance near the Cape Verde Islands when we still had 5000 miles to go and were doing only 50 miles a day, it would seem a completely mad venture and I would think of it with despair. We were like ants trying to climb Mount Everest. Perhaps because I was responsible for the enterprise and the boat was mine, I kept brooding on the number of items damaged or lost and (even if we could patch up something to keep us going), on the difficulty and expense of getting them eventually repaired or replaced. On the other hand as navigator I don't suppose the voyage seemed so long to me as to the others. I regularly saw us getting farther and farther south, then farther and farther east – a dot on the chart, then another and another. The others knew what was happening, but they weren't so close to it; they weren't doing it.

What helped me most was meditation. I had been practising meditation for nearly eight years, and had come to rely on it, particularly in any hardship or setback. Every day during the voyage, at some point I got up on deck forward of the mast, and had half-an-hour to myself. This is no place to go into the benefits of meditation, and how it works is just as much a mystery to me now as when I began. But it does affect one in many different ways and in different aspects of life. Apart from any other benefits, it had the practical advantage that I got away completely for a time from the yacht and its crew, and the crew got away from me.

There were other factors that prevented us feeling too crowded, even after weeks on a 30 ft by 8 ft yacht. We spent most of the afternoon from 1400 to 1800 reading or sleeping to make up for the time we were on watch at night. We always had a convivial drink at sundown and the evening meal was always an occasion. If all was quiet the chap on watch could join us at table or otherwise eat in the cockpit with a plate on his knee. By contrast the night watches were solitary interludes with the stars and moon for company. There is also the constant noise of the sea and the wind which wraps you round. At 15-ft distance you are as alone as if you were a hundred feet away on land. And the noise of wind and waves is pleasant on the whole, though it can be terrifying in a storm. Somehow it doesn't drill into your head like mechanical rackets, nor does it interfere in conversations with those near-by. Finally what makes close companionship more tolerable is that you are all on a journey. The movement, the progress, the fact of going somewhere, is fundamental. Because it is a conveyance, a boat a tenth the size of a house can seem as spacious.

12

IN THE DOLDRUMS

By the eleventh day we were in latitude 13° north and the change of wind from astern to almost ahead meant that we were losing the last of the north-east Trades and moving into the doldrums – or 'tropical convergence zone' as the meteorologists call it. This region round the Equator is popularly associated with calms and hot sun. We experienced these all right, but first we were to run the gauntlet of some tropical cyclones. The first occurred on the eleventh day itself. It was the morning I had been up the mast and fixed the respliced rope halyard. We got under way with the wind east-by-south about Force 4. It was sunny weather with only 20 per cent cloud. For breakfast we had fried eggs, almost the last of them, and for lunch toasted cheese, beans and sausages, with a glass of vermouth.

The storm began to develop in the afternoon. First there were occasional light rain showers. Then to the south and east there grew an enormous black rain cloud that dominated the whole sky. I have never seen anything that looked more formidable. It grew almost pitch dark and coming under this great cloud was like entering a vast dungeon. The sky became the roof of a cavern and the sea an underground river. More ominous still as the boat rode into it, the wind dropped completely. Then it began to pour with rain and there came wind squalls gusting to 35 knots and over. We started to collect the water that was pouring off the mainsail near the mast. We filled container after container until the tanks were full and we had more water than when we left Las Palmas.

Then the wind stopped as suddenly as it had begun. It might have been cut off with a pair of scissors. The boat was picked up and dropped by the confused sea and everything banged wildly about. Once it was almost as if we had dropped into a hole in the sea. Bob was at the tiller and we were wondering if we ought to reduce sail, when suddenly the wind came at us again. If *Swingaway* had been capsizable she would have gone over then. We had no way on, and then suddenly the wind increased from nothing to over 40 knots in a few seconds. It was like a knock-down blow. In the cabin it was pandemonium. Pots and pans, books, tins of food, were all over the place. Fortunately everything spillable or breakable was behind bars or in cupboards. By way of shutting the stable door, we changed to the storm-jib and reefed the mainsail. With the wind the rain fell more heavily than ever. Rain, rain, rain, rain, rain – at 2100, at 2200 it was still streaming down. We were drenched, drowned. It was a deluge that poured steadily into everything: clothes, sleeping bags, even some stores. Despite Bob's work on the cabin ports it found cracks to come in by. Taking the evening and the night together we may have had nine or ten inches of rain.

The contrast between the temperature of the rain and the sea was remarkable. When we were sailing in the rain, and spray came on board, it was like going from the cold tap to the hot tap. While it rained the stifling heat of the past days was gone. Again with the rain the compass light failed and this time, sodden as we were, there was no hope of fixing it in the dark. Finally we gave up, hove to for the night and simply kept a look-out. The morning of the twelfth day brought a red sunrise, a sky covered with grey clouds and drizzling rain. There was a light wind from the south-east and we held a course of 200° by compass, close hauled under full main and genoa. By noon according to the log we were only 46 miles south of our last fix, twenty-four hours before. For breakfast we had boiled eggs and toast with a somewhat peculiar flavour since the bread was by now suffering from mildew. For lunch we had ham, tomatoes, oranges and squash. Our beer had run out the day before.

We had met the storm in a position of 20° 40′ north, 23° 05′ west, some 100 miles off the coast of Gambia, Senegal and Sierra Leone. As part of my colonial service I had spent some years in Freetown where, concentrated in a few months from July to September, the rainfall can reach 200 inches or more. The name Sierra Leone (Lion Mountains) was given by early Portuguese navigators because of the constant growling thunder in these months. Bob found a descriptive passage in the *Africa Pilot*, Vol 1 – 'Other more transitory phenomena are the disturbance lines or line squalls which are experienced in the region south of 20° north ... These thundery squalls which are a distinctive feature of West African weather have sometimes been referred to as tornadoes ... The wind is usually light or calm and the atmosphere is commonly oppressive. As the cloud bank approaches it thickens and darkens . . . A roll formation may sometimes be detected at the base of the cloud, which often assumes the appearance of an arch as it approaches. As the cloud roll passes overhead there is a sudden squall of wind from some easterly direction. On average the wind rises to about 20 to 25 knots but a gust of 50 knots has been recorded. After the onset of the squall, rain commences and is often extremely heavy . . . In general these storms are most frequent near the beginning and end of the wet season.'

The thirteenth day the wind was light but fresh on the quarter and the sun shone. The boat was draped with clothes and bedding drying out. At least it was fresh water. Clothes soaked with salt water have a clammy feel and never get bone dry since the salt attracts moisture again from the atmosphere. But we were soon to get so used to this that we were hardly conscious of it. For a day and a night and a day we made good speed. In the afternoon a cargo boat, the *Delta Paraguay*, steering north-west and very high in the water, passed just a few cables from us. She was the first ship we had seen for four days. The wind backed east and from close-hauled we were again on a reach. There were over 1000 miles on the log with a more respectable 115 miles for the day's run. We were in 8° 59′ north, 22° 43′ west. That evening there were a few rain showers and variable winds which gave us a disturbed night. In light and shifting winds the sails were like fractious children, needing constant attention. In the dark it was impossible to give it, and sometimes we would have been advised to lower everything and go to sleep rather than keep trying to trim them. At night in your bunk you got to know by sound what was happening. Sometimes in light airs they would swish and rustle soft as silk. Sometimes if there was more of a sea they would bang like pistol shots, or claps of thunder as the wind took them one side or the other. These were sounds to keep you awake. It was the creak and groan of steady progress or the trudge of the boat marching onward that would send me to sleep. Also that particular night we passed a steamer at 0345 and we were all out watching as Jack called her up with a torch and asked her to report us to Lloyds.

The next day was as hot as ever. We ran the engine and the alternator belt broke. We fitted a new one but it seemed loose and I wondered if it would last. Because of the heat we decided not to run the engine again in the forenoon, but to try and do it in the coolest part of the day which was about six or seven in the morning. In this fierce sun I spent as much time as I could in the water, in the cabin or in the shade of the sails. I always wore a hat and had a plentiful supply of suncream to block the sun's ultra-violet rays. I needed to take these precautions because of 20 years spent in the tropics which had damaged my skin. One develops 'solar keratoses', horny patches, which if not treated become cancerous. For some years I had been having bits of skin treated, first by surgery, then by cauterising with a red-hot element, then by freezing with liquid nitrogen, as techniques developed. In all three treatments new skin grew in place of the cancerous tissue. On this voyage I had taken every precaution but in the first month I developed a nasty sore caused by too much sun on my lower lip. However I found that the constant salt water was evidently beneficial and, together with my suncream, gradually healed it, especially after we got south of the sun and were going away from it. The sun was strongest in the afternoon. If my trick at the tiller came then, I devised a means of keeping cool yet covered from the sun. I would dip all my clothes – hat, shirt, trousers – in the sea, put them on, and sit there dripping wet and bearably cool, my bare feet tucked under a sail bag. In half-an-hour's time I would be dry again.

On the sixteenth day I wrote in the log: 'The hottest day. Swimming a lot to keep cool.' In the night we had lost a fitting, a heavy stainless-steel slide on the track which led the jib sheet aft. Jack spliced a length of nylon rope into a sling to replace it. Bob fixed the lid of the toolbox whose hinges had rusted and broken off. In light airs we set the spinnaker, then when a rain squall threatened we struck it and set the heavy genoa. Heavy rain fell but this time there was no strong wind. Again we filled the tanks and had more water than ever before. For lunch we had ham, tomatoes, squash and an orange – and because of the rain a cup of soup to start with. Also in the afternoon we had an extra cup of tea. At first tea and coffee made with rain water tasted strange but we soon came to prefer it. Right from the start it tasted better with whisky and made a whisky-water into a new drink. For supper we had sliced roast lamb (from a tin) and a kedgeree of sardines and peas. As we rocked about windless and with a daily run of only 46 miles Jack neatly summed up our frustrations: 'We won't get out of the doldrums until we get some wind. And we won't get any wind until we get out of the doldrums.'

As the days at sea wore on, we lived more and more in a world of skies and clouds and ocean. There were cloudscapes, seascapes, dawns and sunsets, an endless succession of paintings on a gigantic canvas. There would be dark clouds at night, tall fantastic faces in the sky. A long, low cloud on the horizon was for all the world like a great serpent with the sun for its eye. Like Hamlet we saw figures in the clouds and as well as a camel and a whale there was a huge clown, a black dog and many more. Dawns and sunsets were made more of texture and colour than shapes. One striking dawn began with flocks of small clouds high in the east, turning pink then red. Then the sun's disc, a golden coin, came up over the edge of the sea, and as it rose the sky turned blue and white with golden hues low on the horizon. In 29° south on the Greenwich meridian after a stormy day came one of those dramatic red sunsets that promise better weather. In part of the west were angry, flame-coloured clouds in hard layers like slabs of rock, but to offset them were masses of softest cotton-wool shading from light pink into a fiery centre.

At night another world surrounded us. The moon was with us in all her changing shapes and sizes. Sometimes her broad features would beam benignly on our progress. Once, just risen, slightly oval in shape, resting on clouds, she was like a golden egg in its nest. She might be a round silver penny, a lemon-coloured lozenge, a lump of cheese, a sliver of finger-nail. There was the half moon, lying on her back, a cradle for the stars. Sometimes the night would start without her and the stars would shine like magic lamps. But they would all grow pale as the moon rose and flooded the sky. One night she was so big and clear as to light the horizon for a sight and let me read the sextant by her own brightness. At another time, a white ghost in the sky with the sun, she gave us a second observation and a crossing position line, to give us our exact whereabouts.

On the eighteenth day a noon sight put us 4° 44′ north, but I got no morning or evening sights because of cloud. There were more showers and very variable winds with squalls. Bob lost a notebook overboard. I noticed that small barnacles were beginning to grow on the floats. We collected a few cups of water but our tanks were full with enough water for perhaps eighty days. The bread was finished and we had started on tins of biscuit. So were the eggs. Several we had had to throw away because they were bad. We still had plenty of tinned food even for the 4500 miles we still had to go. That night for supper we had beefburgers, haricot beans, mashed potatoes, peaches and a glass of wine.

Though we were so near the line, the tropical squalls were not finished yet. The next day a morning sight, azimuth 92°, put us on 22° 06′ west, but instead of noonday sun there was drizzling rain. In the morning between showers there was a perfect rainbow stretching right across the sky to the east, but far from being a sign of better weather, we had as much rain after it as before. In the morning Jack fixed the stern light which had failed two nights before. He found it was corroded when he unscrewed the cover. It went when he put a new bulb in, but we were to have further trouble. We tried to account for discrepancies over the past ten days between the day's run on the Electra log and the sun sights. We thought the log might be under-reading, but though we had no Walker log to compare it with, it seemed perfectly all right when we brought it inboard (it was fitted through the bottom of the hull) and examined it. Then two days later it stopped. Bob got it going again by cleaning the earth and reconnecting it, so perhaps it had been working intermittently.

That night black clouds built up again and once more we seemed to be entering the infernal regions. Again they were huge rain clouds holding what must have been tons of water. We had a worrying, disturbed night. Winds up to Force 6 or 7, then no wind, wind from the south, from the north, from the east, from the west. In the morning we were tossing in a violent, confused sea. All night it had rained, by noon it was still raining. This was the twentieth day from Las Palmas and we had been in this zone of calms and storms for nine days. By 1600 the rain was heavier than ever and the wind was gusting to 35 knots. With a big sea, we decided to reduce sail and started to reef the main, when the wind moderated. That night was more peaceful. There were still showers but the sea was smoother. The next day, the twenty-first, the log showed only 145 miles for the past three days. For three days we had got no sun sights, but we hoped we were near the line. That afternoon I got sights which put us 22° 08′ west and 1° 50′ north. It was still 100 miles to the Equator.

13

ACROSS THE LINE

THAT afternoon a steady breeze sprang up from the south, and close hauled we could make a compass course of 240° which with a magnetic variation of 20° gave us a true course of 220°. Our speed went from 2 to 3 to 4 knots. At last it seemed we might be catching the south-east Trades. We had a good night and made steady progress. The fair breeze continued the next day and we were making a good 5 knots, steering 240° to 210° It was fine sunny weather with a different, crisper feeling in the atmosphere.

On *Swingaway* the mainsail was cut with a string running down the leech to hold the after edge of the sail taut. It was a detail I didn't pay enough attention to, or check to see the cord was not allowed too much play. Over the weeks of sailing it slackened and with the slight play had chafed through. As so often happened, it went during the night, and the broken cord pulled right out through the sail, so there was no possibility of using the old cord to pull a new one through. A new cord would have to be re-threaded from scratch. The after four inches of the sail was flogging badly as we went to windward and it was clear that before many days sailing, the after edge of the sail would be in tatters.

Jack was the expert on rope work and sail repairs. The problem was to thread a new cord through a 35-foot hem in stiff, heavy canvas, without any proper tools. Jack hesitated over the job as if he didn't want to do it.

'We'll all lend a hand,' I said to encourage him. 'It shouldn't take more than half-an-hour.'

In the end it took us half a day and frayed all our tempers. We made up a bodkin of heavy copper wire doubled to make an eye for the cord, which had to be good strong nylon. The first time we threaded the cord loosely through the copper. After about 10 feet it pulled out. We had to work the bodkin back and start again. Then we tried tying the cord to the bodkin with a knot, but after only 5 or

6 feet the knot stuck fast. Then we doubled the cord back through the bodkin and sewed it to itself with linen thread. This worked well for the first 10 feet or so but it got progressively harder to pull the cord through the sail. After 15 feet it refused to budge unless we stretched the sail completely straight. The problem then was that whereas the boat was only 30 feet long, the edge of the sail was 5 feet longer. Somehow, fingers sore and nails broken, we managed inch by inch, one at the stern, one at the bow, one amidships. Then 1 foot from the peak, the copper wire bent and stuck immovably.

'Let's cut the bloody thing out,' said Jack, and I agreed though it hurts to cut a perfectly good sail. So we cut the bodkin out and led the cord up the last foot outside the hem. The sail certainly wouldn't flog so near the head. When we got it out, the strong copper wire was twisted almost into knots. The job over, we spliced the main-brace, and had the satisfaction of seeing the mainsail set perfectly again. Although we had lost nearly half a day's sailing, there was still cause for satisfaction. The noon sight put us 0° 22' north, only 22 miles to the Equator. We would cross that evening.

Despite having been so long in the Navy, I don't think Jack had crossed the line before. Bob had only flown across but was excited at the prospect of seeing the Southern Cross again. I thought back to crossing-the-line ceremonies I had enjoyed on board passenger ships. Neptune would come over the rail with a long beard and a trident, splash the shrieking lady passengers, and in the swimming-pool duck a junior member of the crew dressed as a mermaid with long, blond tresses and lipstick an inch thick. Nowadays crossing by plane has become an uncelebrated non-event with rows of sleepy passengers half-watching a film.

We had a celebration dinner. I got out one of our three bottles of champagne, we opened a tin containing a whole chicken cooked in wine, and with peas, celery and potatoes, asparagus to start and pancakes in rum to follow, we dined a thousand miles from anywhere, as well as if we had been at the Ritz. Though I must say I'd have given a lot for a green salad to go with it.

The next day, the twenty-third from Las Palmas, it was cooler, we had a fresh breeze and we looked forward to a week or more of sailing on the same tack, running close hauled down the edge of the south-east Trades. The sun's meridian passage gave us 1° 22' south and we were 24° 45' west. Though we were south of the Equator, the sun was still south of us (it was Sunday 30 September and autumn in the Northern Hemisphere), and still, as it were, travelling south at 15′ of arc (or 15 miles on the earth's surface) a day.

During the night there was a slight accident that was to lead to a bigger one. *Swingaway* had a kicking-strap for the boom that was new to me. It was a bottle-screw fixed to the boom a foot behind the goose-neck and fixed to the mast a foot below the goose-neck. Since it was fairly loose when I took over the boat, and the mainsail set perfectly well on all points of sailing without its help, I had left it alone. If we were using the mainsail for prolonged running we usually held the boom down by a line from the after end to one of the floats. This held the sail flatter, damped the bouncing of the boom in a lively sea, and was a safeguard against an accidental gybe.

Now, however, with so many weeks' movement of the boom, the bottle-screw came undone in the night and the middle section seemed to have gone overboard. Then later in the day Jack found the barrel in the scuppers and proceeded to set it up. He screwed it bar-tight, and my suggestion that some play should be left in it was not especially welcomed. He muttered something about everything being slack and gave a few extra turns with the spanner. Not wanting to make an issue of it, I dropped the matter. But I felt uneasy about it and a couple of days later I took the opportunity of being alone on deck to ease it off. Unfortunately Jack noticed it and with the rhetorical question, 'Who's been buggering about with this?' set it up bar-tight again. I thought if I insisted it might blow up into a row quite out of proportion, so I let it go. Perhaps I should have been tougher because it was to cause us more trouble.

The twenty-fourth day we ran the engine, which went well with no trouble from the belt. With no stray flying fish we had tinned beans, biscuits, marmalade and coffee for breakfast; for lunch, ham and tinned salad. The oranges we had brought from Las Palmas were finished and for Vitamin C we began to take a daily tot of bottled unsweetened lemon juice. Besides solitaire we had started playing chess, and this particular day Bob saw me off with a nicely combined mate. Jack would only play occasionally and could mount some devastating attacks, but if one played patiently on the defensive he sometimes gave the game away. We all played cards too. Single-handed patience games, various two-handed games, and sometimes three-handed poker, *vingt-et-un*, rummy, whist or bridge. I got help from the others with my crossword clues. On this particular day I reached Puzzle 94 in the *Daily Telegraph* book, with the book of *Guardian* crosswords still in hand. So we passed the time agreeably enough. For supper we had pea soup, the rest of the ham and tinned salad, and a rice pudding made on board with salt water. The first time we tried this it was too salty to eat, but using a mixture with less water, Jack managed to turn out something that to our keen appetites tasted rather good.

As we travelled south, the stars in the night sky were changing. The Southern Cross came up above the horizon ahead of us, though it was some time before I could pick it out straight away. We had a star-finder consisting of plastic circles with a grid, which from the star's Siderial Hour Angle and declination gave its approximate height and bearing. It was difficult to use at night as it was complicated to sort out the right discs and put them together, and the names and measurements were small and hard to read without a good light. It was best to work out beforehand during the day the bearing and height of particular stars at a particular hour, and then be ready to look for them when night came. But we rarely had the time or energy to prepare in advance. I never got to know all the stars, there were too many of them, but I made the acquaintance of half-a-dozen and a planet or two as well. The big, bright stars with low declination kept us company all the way – Rigel, Betelgeuse, Bellatrix, Sirius and the rest. But we lost the Plough or Charles's Wain. 'The Plough is gone. Perhaps I'll never see it again,' said Jack.

The twenty-fourth and twenty-fifth days from Las Palmas saw us almost directly underneath the sun. In fact on the twenty-fourth day the sun's distance from the zenith at meridian passage was only 02' (or two miles on the earth's surface). This had two curious effects. First, it was as easy to bring the sun down to the horizon with the sextant to the north as to the south. Second, the sun's bearing at meridian passage from east to west changed rapidly. When brought down to sea level, the sun circled the horizon from due east to due west in the few minutes it took to pass overhead, and the second when it was bearing due south (or north) was the exact time of its passage overhead. We had got good radio reception that morning so I had the time of meridian passage, 13h. 31m. 24s. GMT, right to within seconds. Normally with a noon sight you observe the sun's altitude rising to a maximum, 'standing' or 'hanging' for a second or two and then falling. This apparent movement right round the horizon was far more obvious and dramatic.

Now that we were on a beat and continuously on the same tack, the self-steering vane was working twenty-four hours a day without much attention. From the twentieth day we had had it easy and it transformed both the nights and days. For twenty days before that we had been continuously at the helm, and even divided by three the physical and mental effort and the inconvenience in not being able to leave it became a hardship. On the twenty-fifth day the log again showed less distance run than the sun sights. There was 30 miles difference, which seems a lot, even though we had found the log had stopped twice. Bob cleaned the impeller hoping this would improve its performance.

From the twenty-fifth day the Trades got stronger and we began a series of good daily runs – 110 miles, then 117, 132, 112, 103, 122, 125, and 119. Some days there was a big sea with the boat pitching into it forcefully. On the twenty-fifth day we were in longitude 26° 37′ west and still having to steer slightly west because of the wind. The next two days saw us in longitude 27° west and 27° 11′ west. That was our farthest west longitude. We were the same latitude as Recife in Brazil, and only three days' sail away. Nevertheless we carried on. From the twenty-seventh day we were able to steer 180° magnetic and with each 100 miles farther south, still more to the east, 180° to 170°. Then with the wind lighter and drawing ahead we had to go back to 200°. Soon again we were steering 195° then 180°. Finally on day thirty-one in 17° south, we could steer 150° to 170°. By then our longitude was 24° 52′ west. Gradually we were easing over towards South Africa.

On some days taking sights was difficult. First I would put sun cream on my face, especially on my sore lower lip, because you can't avoid facing the sun. Then even on good days I would climb on the cabin top holding the sextant as carefully as a collector's piece of porcelain. The extra height of the cabin top seemed to give a better view and a better horizon, though sometimes the sails got in the way. I would shout 'Now' for Bob or Jack to write down the time from the watch, then take a rest and relax before another concentrated effort. We always took at least five readings and averaged them out. On bad days it was even more like trying to hold a glass of water steady while riding a cantering horse. It could be a real problem keeping the sextant steady and sighting the sun on the horizon. I found it best to have my legs wedged firmly and my body free to go with the boat's motion. The other difficulty was with spray on the sextant, and just as bad, on my glasses. In the very roughest conditions it meant giving up.

On the thirtieth day we were in longitude 26° 04′ west, 15° south and had over 2,500 miles on the log. Despite good recent progress, because of the calms and delays of the tropics we had averaged well under 100 miles a day. But now I could spend the afternoon watch looking at *Swingaway* sail herself. It was a fine sight. In Force 5 to 6, a point or two free of the wind, she took the swell at an angle and mostly very comfortably. The log showed 4 to 5 to 6 knots, and steering by the wind the compass was showing 160°, 150° and even occasionally 140°, so that with 25° west variation, we were going well to the east. Sometimes there would be a bang and she would lose way meeting a wave head on. On this long stretch pitching to windward, the two forward bunks must have been uncomfortable at times, but neither Bob nor Jack complained, and both seemed to sleep as soundly as in a feather-bed ashore.

After nearly five weeks at sea we were all reasonably fit. Jack got occasional headaches and Bob complained of constipation. Apart from my sore lip I developed a backache which I decided was caused by standing and balancing against the pitch and roll of the boat. I sat and lay as much as possible and it went away. We got no more rain on board and our water ration was only just adequate: a mug for breakfast, a mug for lunch, and a mug for tea – just over a pint. There was some juice from tinned vegetables and fruit, and we were allowed a little water if we chose to have rum, gin or whisky in the evening. Because of their dehydrating effect we gradually drank less and less of spirits. Rum being the sweetest was the best, but both beer and wine were more popular. The beer ran out on the tenth day and the wine on the fiftieth. There were times when one longed for more liquid, and I would spend some night watches obsessed with the thought of a glass of water. Once or twice the temptation to steal even half a cup while the others were asleep needed real determination to resist. Whether the other two felt it as strongly I never knew. It was a subject we didn't discuss. Towards the end we had lost weight and were no doubt suffering from dehydration. We weren't dying of thirst, but I could at least picture what it would be like. The image of a desert traveller crawling in the sand with lolling tongue and haggard eyes raised to heaven isn't a figment of the novelist's imagination.

On the twenty-eighth day we had noticed some clicking in the after port girder where it was bolted to the main hull. This time (unlike the kicking strap) I had no doubt it should be really tight. We worked round the bolts with a spanner but failed to eliminate it entirely. Five days later, by the thirty-third day, the noise was worse and if we put a hand to touch the hull and the girder, we could feel movement. The wind was less and we decided to spend a morning doing a more thorough job. We lowered the sails and lay ahull, while Bob and I unscrewed everything and put in new rubber washers. Early on we lost a small screwdriver overboard. After that when working outboard we had a line tied to the tools and round the wrist. We were especially careful with the precious last spanner. If that went we could do nothing. In tightening up we gave it everything we could, and even put a line on the spanner to get more purchase. In the end we eliminated the clicking entirely. There was also the faintest possible click in the starboard forward girder where it joined the main hull. Again we changed the rubbers and tightened up to the maximum, but couldn't eliminate the last faint sound. However, we kept careful check every day for the rest of the voyage and it got no worse.

While Bob and I were busy with the float girders, Jack cleaned barnacles off the rudder. During spells from other chores I also cleaned some off the floats. They had got much bigger and they were hard to get off. There were more under the waterline and it would take a long session to clear them. The work cost us two or three hours' sailing and that afternoon we were depressingly becalmed. For lunch we had beans, sardines, pickled onions and lemon juice; for supper, steak-and-kidney pudding, peas and mashed potatoes, with a glass of wine and a tin of pineapple to follow. Bob took sights of two planets – Venus and Jupiter – and worked out a position farther west and south than my sun sights. However, as it was his first star sight and the telescope wasn't too good at night, he reckoned his results were more in doubt.

14

Beyond the South-East Trades

Now we had lost the Trades we were to have days of frustrating calms, and low mileages again. On successive days our daily run was 80, 68, 30, 55 and 42 miles. On the thirty-fifth day after a windless night we were completely becalmed, the sea like glass, the sails not even flapping in the still air. We spent the morning taking off the rest of the barnacles. I had a diving mask and snorkel on board which made the work easier. Bob was the strongest diver and cleared most of the barnacles far under the hull. Finally we got it all clean except for some in the centre-board casing. I wondered if barnacles would make an addition to our diet and I tried boiling some in salt water, but they were so tough and rubbery I threw them away.

Swingaway had become our home and the outside world was remote. We had not seen another ship for three weeks. But we heard most of the news except when reception was too bad, when even the BBC was reduced to crackling voices and the faint pips of a time signal. We were listening when the Arabs attacked Israel. It was the beginning of a war that was followed by an oil crisis, chaos in Britain and world-wide inflation. Although we listened intently to each day's news and followed the fluctuations of the fighting, we hardly thought it would affect us.

'Nobody's going to drop an atomic bomb here,' said Jack.

But when it came to repairs and replacements for the boat, the delays and difficulties were to be that much worse.

However, until we reached land we were immune. More important were the duties of the day: Bob cooking a pie for the evening or working on the engine, or the compass; Jack splicing a rope or tuning in on one of the radios; me taking a sight or pouring out the drinks. While we had been sailing through the Trades it had still been hot in the cabin, but cool enough on deck. Now we had more hot days with beating sun, better for swimming or lying about than doing chores.

I had finished the *Telegraph* puzzles, done the first few *Guardian* crosswords, and was getting on with Shakespeare. *Coriolanus*, I thought, had no love interest but would act well with a big, powerful actor. What a contrast was *Titus Andronicus* with its rank melodrama, its extremes of sex and violence. *Pericles* was a romantic fantasy of shipwreck, supposed death, marvellous survival and coincidental reunion. The light comedy of *Cymbeline* with its betting on the heroine's virtue had a similar theme to *Così Fan Tutte*. It was too full of inconsistencies and contrivance, but what a charming heroine. I ploughed my way through *Love's Labour Lost* and found *Troilus and Cressida* depressing, as I did *Timon of Athens* with its Barmecide feast and ruined Croesus who 'all living men did hate'. But the tricks and turns of *Two Gentlemen of Verona* kept me reading by the light of the Tilley lamp. This may seem a digression in the story of a sailing voyage. But Shakespeare has something to say about everything, and I came across a good half-dozen passages to do with sailing and the sea. Here for instance is the fisherman from *Pericles* ' . . . said I not as much when I saw the porpas how he bounc'd and tumbled? They say they're half fish, half flesh . . . ' The description of their motion in the sea is not only vivid but exact, and since they are aquatic mammals they are indeed 'half fish, half flesh'.

On occasions the porpoises and dolphins would jump right out of the water. Their colouring was interesting too. Like many sea birds and fish their colouring is light below and dark above. On top they were dark blue or brown, almost black, but underneath a light greenish grey. In some cases this colouring must be for camouflage, the light belly seen from below merging with the sky, the dark back seen from above invisible against the darkness of the sea. But apart from man, who are the enemies of the porpoises and dolphins? Not sharks; for they are said to attack sharks by butting them until they are stunned and causing them to drown. Perhaps they are attacked by killer whales. We never saw sharks when there were dolphins about. We did see a school of whales and dolphins together, but I have no idea whether the whales were chasing the dolphins.

On the thirty-sixth day one of the winches jammed. There was no means of taking it to pieces or oiling it, but we took it off and soaked it in paraffin. There were two big winches on either side of the cockpit so we could still handle the sheets. In any case with a lot of working the stiffness gradually got easier. The next day I found a hole in the foot of the light genoa where it flapped against the guard rail in light airs. The foot of all the three jibs needed attention. I tried sticking tape along the foot of the genoa on both sides, but it came off when the sail was used. It needed a proper sewing job and would have to wait until we got to Cape Town.

We tried to make the best of the light airs and changeable conditions, by setting as much sail as the boat could carry comfortably, changing from working jib, to heavy genoa, to light genoa, to spinnaker, and back again, as the wind fell or increased, or veered or backed, and blew from ahead, from astern or from the beam. Though it increased our speed by a knot or more and could be used for reaching, the spinnaker was a troublesome sail, collapsing in light airs, needing constant trimming, and an eye always on the weather to avoid the danger of carrying it too long. One of its annoying habits was to wrap itself round the forestay. It only needed a moment's inattention at the tiller and a slight shift of wind. It would start from the peak and unless it was unwrapped straight away would get worse and worse. The stronger the wind the harder it was to unwrap and we had many a struggle with it. Finally (I think it was Bob's suggestion) we carried the jib set as well and with the fore triangle filled by another sail the spinnaker behaved better.

By the thirty-ninth day we were in 15° 53′ west, 25° 25′ south, we had covered 3,200 miles and were steering 140° on a reach with the wind slightly aft of the beam. It was a cloudy day, the barometer 1025 millibars, the temperature 70° Fahrenheit at 0800. That night there were no stars visible and a clouded moon. We had a few showers and heavier rain at breakfast time. I got no morning sight, but we collected two saucepans of fresh water. It wasn't the abundance from heaven we had had in earlier rainstorms but it was still a gift from the gods. Cooks and housewives who dread metering today can't imagine what it meant to us. For lunch we had sausages, savoury rice, carrots and pineapple; for supper a stew of mint-flavoured lamb, mashed potatoes made from powder, and vegetables, with a glass of wine and tinned peaches. That evening we found the bilges rather full and it took 170 strokes to clear them. We put it down to the rain. I had temporarily given up Shakespeare and was reading the *Acts of the Apostles*. What a terse, graphic account of the spread of Christianity and with what memorable phrases: ' "Then", said Paul, "I stand at Caesar's judgement seat ... I appeal unto Caesar." ' I had certainly chosen books about the sea, for a highlight of *Acts* is the account of Paul's shipwreck on

Malta after fourteen days at sea. It is interesting to compare this with Ulysses' shipwreck in the *Odyssey* when sailing single-handed from Calypso's island to Phaeacia. One is all gods, poetry, magic invention and fantasy; the other an almost dry, matter-of-fact report, it might be 'News-at-ten, Malta'. Is it the difference between ancient and modern, or between Greece and Rome, or simply between the writer of the *Acts* and Homer?

On the forty-first day we set the spinnaker at 0745 (we never carried it at night) as the wind was more astern, almost north-west. We were running comfortably in a Force 4 wind, doing 4 to 6 knots and the weather seemed to have cleared. Then at 1050 there was cloud to windward and a line of rain advanced towards us, but not it seemed, with alarming rapidity. Then in less than a minute the wind increased from 12 knots to 24, from 24 knots to 35. We looked like losing the spinnaker and with Bob at the tiller I got to the halyard while Jack was at the bow, ready to spill the wind and gather the sail in as I eased it down. Mostly I used gloves for handling sheets but this time it had been too much of a rush. I started to ease the halyard, keeping several turns round the mast winch to control it. But I was confused by the pouring rain. I misjudged the force of the wind and the rope got away from me. Like a fool I tried to hold it, and it chewed up my hands. The top of the spinnaker blew out, hauling the halyard right through the block at the top of the mast, and the sail fell on top of Jack, who emerged with a sour look until he saw my hands. Fortunately it didn't go under the boat and we were able to gather it in and stow it. I lost the skin off four finger-tips on my right hand and two on my left, and had three rope burns on the palms. In five minutes the squall was over, the wind back to 12 knots, and I thought glumly that if we had simply left the spinnaker, everything would probably have held. In the confusion we also lost overboard a saucepan, which had been brought up to collect water.

I wasn't suffering with shock from my hands. I get more upset if there is a lot of blood about. With no shock they weren't so painful immediately, and therefore with my hands well taped, I decided to go up the mast and re-reeve the missing halyard. After all it was my fault. Jack took the tiller and Bob hauled me up. There was a fair swell running, but I went up on the wire jib-halyard which Jack had so painfully respliced, and as we left the mainsail set, I got some shelter and a feeling of greater security than on a bare pole. Soon after, we hoisted the spinnaker again, but lowered it at 1155 when another squally cloud appeared. This time the increase was not so rapid or dramatic, but by 1300 we had gusts up to 32 knots. Thereafter the breeze settled down to a steadier 16 to 20 knots. This time there was no rain-shower and we got no more fresh water.

The bilge was still making water and for the second time that day we pumped 30 to 40 strokes. We went over all the fittings through the hull – echo-sounder, electric log, stopcocks for the WC, centreboard casing, engine water intake. They were all OK and it seemed the stern gland of the propeller was the most probable source of the trouble.

The previous night the log had fouled twice. This was extraordinary after sixty days at sea without any trouble from it, and the cause was out of the ordinary too. Caught round the shaft of the little impeller were strings perhaps four inches long, made of some stuff like very strong spider web. The strings were a vivid blue colour and seemed to contain eggs, presumably of some fish. From then on for more than ten days, our days and night watches were occupied with cleaning the log of these strings. There must have been millions of them over a thousand miles of sea. If the steering was tricky and we couldn't leave the helm, we had to wait until the next man came on watch. Though we added some mileage based on our speed and on the time the log was not working, the record of our daily run was somewhat uncertain. Jack put some of the eggs into a cup of sea water to see if they would hatch, but a rough spell of weather upset it.

On the forty-second day I pumped the bilges 90 strokes and Bob tightened the stern gland, crawling past the engine to get at it. He also checked the batteries and ran the engine. With much hammering into place, our wooden plug for the exhaust had split, and we cut another bung out of softwood. During the day we had travelling clouds, some showers and a big following sea. I was glad we were not going into these enormous waves for the swell was bigger than anything I had seen anywhere else. From then on, this majestic swell was with us for much of the time.

My hands were fairly comfortable and looked as though they would heal quickly if I could keep them dry. The morning sight put us 9° 28′ west and at noon our latitude was about 28° south. (There was a lot of movement in the boat and the horizon was a bad one.) Bob took an evening sight which put us on 8° 50′ west. Since the days of calm we had been making better time. From day thirty-eight our daily mileages were 96, 98, 101, 106, 132 and 127. If we had always had runs like this, we would by that time have been in Cape

Town. As it was we still had another 6° south to go, and still had to make more than 26° of Easting.

At 0730 on the morning of the next day, quite by chance and with reception better than usual, I heard a talk by a friend on BBC radio. He was a film critic, Gordon Gow, and we had met at press shows. He was from Sydney and besides our interest in cinema, we had in common that we were both from the Antipodes and were both keen ballet and opera-goers. His talk was one of a BBC series *Focus on Film*, and it was fascinating to listen to a succinct, witty account of the artificial Garbo-Cukor-Dietrich-Sternberg world of the Hollywood Thirties, in the cabin of a small boat, tossing about thousands of miles from anywhere. I sat down and wrote him a postcard addressed from 6° 34′ west, 28° 13′ south to tell him how much I had enjoyed his talk, and posted it to him later in Cape Town.

The next day we were still on a broad beat, but gradually by midday the wind backed so that we were almost close hauled, with centre-board down, steering 130°. Within the space of a week the wind had gone right round – from south-east through east, north, west, south, and now south-east again. The bilges were much drier; Bob's work seemed to have cured the leak. But there were other running repairs. Part of the apparatus for the wind-vane self-steering was a bicycle chain fitted round a large cog on the tiller, which made small adjustments possible. Our weeks at sea had gummed it up so it would hardly move. Nursing my hands, I took it off, washed it in paraffin and oiled it well. I also mended a tear in my oilskins with Evostick (it stood up well) and sewed a button on my anorak. We were having trouble with the forward hatch cover since the catch, a small brass bolt, had broken. It didn't shut tightly enough and if there was any weather, rain and spray found their way in. As a temporary measure we rigged up a piece of shock cord to hold it shut. Jack made a cake for tea with flour, sugar, dried milk, cocoa and cooking oil. It was halfway between a cake and a biscuit and not for those with weak jaws, but it tasted good. We had hash for supper.

15
TROUBLE AT SEA

THAT night at about 2045 it was dark, the wind was Force 6, we were close hauled and Jack was at the tiller. Through trying to sail too close or through inattention, he came up into the wind without meaning to, and got caught in irons. Like many multihulls, *Swingaway* was awkward going about because she was so light on the water. She lost way quickly and you could very soon find her moving backwards and have to apply reverse tiller. When tacking, it paid to ease the main sheet, let her pay off slightly to increase speed and, after the helm had been put over, hold the jib aback to carry the bow round, then bring in the jib-sheet on the other tack with the wind on it. It meant hard work on the winch and it was easier for two than for one.

When I heard Jack having to manoeuvre I went out to give him a hand. Usually with two it was easy enough to get back on the right tack and on course again. This time, however, nothing seemed to serve. We backed the jib, we let the boat pay off. It seemed she wouldn't sail. Having just come out of the bright cabin, I couldn't see properly and I got a torch. There was the boom pointing up at a right angle. Clear enough in the torch beam, the main boom was *broken*! The metal had fractured right across at the kicking-strap. I felt devastated.

Freeing the main sheet to ease going about had allowed the wind on the main sail to lift the boom. A tight leech string may have been a factor, but the main cause had been screwing down the kicking-strap to its limit. I cursed myself for letting it happen. Jack looked a bit grim and didn't say anything. Very likely there had been a strain on the boom for days without our noticing, and this was simply the culmination. A broken boom. At the time it seemed the ultimate disaster. We would do something – but what?

'Don't worry, we'll fix it tomorrow,' said Bob, practical as ever. There was nothing we could do that night. We got the mainsail down straight away; the sail itself was not damaged or torn along the foot. That at least was something to be thankful for. We lowered the jib and lay ahull for the night. We all turned in and for almost the first time since the voyage started, kept no night watches. It was a luxury and consoled us all, to have a whole night in our bunks without interruption. I looked out a few times. We were lying easily enough beam on to the wind, drifting north-west at, say, a quarter of a knot. The wind had got up to Force 7, it was a rough night and I was glad just to poke my nose out and get back to a warm bunk. Though I didn't know it, we had a worrying, uncomfortable time ahead.

We were in longitude 5° west, and I had in mind for some days that we should go on to South African time, which was two hours ahead of GMT. For the whole of the voyage so far we had been on GMT, which had a certain convenience for time signals and navigation. South African time would correspond at least as well with the sun, would give us a lighter evening, and would be an encouraging sign that we were getting nearer our goal. Now was the time to change as we had had an easy night, and we would have longer daylight if we needed it for working on the boom.

We got up at 0500 then and changed our watches to 0700. After breakfast we got to work on the broken boom which had been lashed down for the night. First we eased the mainsail carefully out of the track. It ran along held by a rope sewn along the foot of the sail. The main boom was hollow, made of the same anodised bronze metal as the mast, and its lateral strength was thus limited. If it had been an old-fashioned boom of solid wood it would have held. The only way to mend it effectively was to put a splint down the middle. Nothing could be fixed securely on the outside (the tins we had used for the spinnaker-pole were too small) and anything round the boom would prevent the mainsail sliding along the track. Bob took charge of the operation and proposed using the long end of the spinnaker-pole which was already broken, as a splint. It had broken not far from one end, and with some wooden wedges would make a tight fit. We dismantled the splint we had already put on the spinnaker-pole, took all the fittings off the long end and tried it inside the boom. Then we padded the gaps with a wooden broom-handle and some long pieces of timber until it was a tight fit, and began the slow business of knocking together the two broken ends. Slowly, using a thick slab of wood as a mallet, we forced the two ends together inch by inch. At one point I thought we had got it too tight and it would stick fast with a gap between the broken ends. This would have spoiled everything as we could never have pulled it apart. In the end it came together and the broken ends met exactly. We had already filed the jagged edges of the track, and the foot of the mainsail slid in without difficulty.

By 1100 we had it ready. We had a break and a coffee with rum to toast Bob's ingenuity. The weather had been steadily getting worse and now it was blowing really hard and we would have to reef, especially if we were trying to nurse the mended boom. To use the roller reefing we had first to hoist the full sail and this proved impossible. It flogged so badly that one of the batten pockets tore off and we lost the batten. Also it was shaking the boom so badly we were apprehensive. At Jack's suggestion we tried a jury-rig using the working jib hoisted as a loose-footed mainsail, and the storm jib set forrad. The wind was a good Force 7 to 8, blowing from the south-east, from dead ahead. Under this rig *Swingaway* would hardly go to windward at all. The best we could do was well north of east or west of south, neither of them courses that would take us to Cape Town. Finally we settled down for a time to steering 220° compass and making 2½ knots into an enormous sea. It was miserable wet work.

After lunch (sausage rolls and a tin of peas) we thought of using the emergency reef points on the mainsail instead of the roller reefing. Then we would be able to tie the sail down before we hoisted it, which would be better for the sail and better for the boom. By 1600 we had it up, it set reasonably well, our speed went up to 3 or 4 knots and we pointed better. Because of the lost batten the leech of the main began to flog, but we were able to quieten it by pulling the leech string down tighter. All evening and all that night we pitched into a howling wind and a huge swell. We were steering 210° south by the compass on the port tack or 184° true, as we could only make a course north of east on the starboard tack. Towards morning the wind veered to the south and we went on to the starboard tack, steering 130°.

It was a sleepless night. This was the worst storm we had had, and having to beat right into it made it all the worse. *Swingaway* groaned, shuddered, protested, ploughed on. Sometimes at the top of a wave she would pitch over and come down with a sickening thud, jarring everything. There was water leaking into the cabin through the forward hatchway, the chimney of the oil heater, and the cabin daylights. The cockpit might just as well have been under water. Everything was clammy and cold. In the morning watch the sheet of the storm jib shook free. We lowered the sail before it could flog to bits, but it took two of us to rehoist it and sheet it in. We lost part of a torch overboard and got the halyard foul round the mast.

I tried to take a morning sight but though the sun appeared, there was too much spray. I got the sextant and myself thoroughly soaked and gave up in disgust. After breakfast we managed to change from the storm jib to the working jib and our speed increased to six knots. Again it was too rough to take a sight of the sun at meridian passage. At least a flying fish had come on board, so I had it for lunch while the others had ham. We carried on crashing into a huge sea with all the time violent movement, howling wind, and every now and then a big bang. At times the wind was gusting to nearly 50 knots. We heard on the radio that Chay Blyth was leading the first leg of the Whitbread Round-the-World Race and was expected in Cape Town the next day. In fact the first boat didn't get in until five days later.

By 1700 ship's time, the wind had moderated to 35 knots but the sea was still tremendous. We pumped the bilges 200 strokes, and hoped it was all spray that had come through the hatch or the cabin. Anything in the cockpit or running along the scuppers drained back into the sea. At 1600, taking a distance run by the log, our DR position was 4° 25' west, 29° 40' south. At 1750 we could get no reading from the wind gauge, the expensive and elegant instrument that decorated the mast. I crawled forward and found that it had simply disappeared. We found afterwards that the heavy screws fixing it to a plate on top of the mast had been wrenched from their sockets. I don't think the wind had actually blown it away. I put it down to the violent pitching which had gone on for two days now, and at the top of the mast would be magnified many times. The wind gauge was something we could do without, but we had come to rely on it and sail by it and would miss it. It was another minor blow. Again we had a miserable night, worse than the previous one since all our gear was getting progressively wetter. There is nothing more discouraging than to come off watch after three hours in the dark, flailed by wind and spray in the cockpit, and then have to crawl into a soaking sleeping bag.

The next day, 23 October, was our forty-sixth day from Las Palmas. There were still big seas and strong winds from the south. We were still close hauled on the starboard tack steering 150° compass. During the morning the wind and sea got up again. Without a gauge we could not measure the wind speed, but I reckon it was a good Force 10. The log showed our speed as 8 knots and in the enormous swell I got worried about the boat, thinking if we carried too much canvas, the combination of big waves and strong winds might turn her over. The boom seemed all right and close hauled the main sheet held it down tightly. It had developed a very slight bend, but not enough to affect the set of the sail, and only evident if one looked carefully.

To be on the safe side we changed down from the working jib back to the storm jib. Our speed dropped to 4 knots and the motion was still violent, but at least there was no fear of capsize. After we set the storm jib a shackle came off the luff of the sail, but Bob crawled up to the bow and sewed it on again. We had some of our fresh water stored in 5-gallon plastic containers in a well on the fo'c'sle which held the anchor and cable. Everything had been well lashed down, but after changing sails I thought I ought to have a thorough check. What I found was not encouraging. Of the three containers, one had either worked or broken free of its lashing and gone overboard. A second container had chafed against the fluke of the anchor, there was a hole in the plastic and it was empty. The cap of the third container had come loose and it was only half full. Slowly and painfully I dragged it back to the cockpit. We had used much of the 50 gallons in the main tanks and had a 5-gallon container lashed to the binnacle ready to go over with the life raft in an emergency. That was all we had, and in this region we could not rely on collecting much from rain. It was all bad news, but it was nobody's fault in particular and there were no recriminations – it was just one of those things. We decided, at least until we were nearer Cape Town, to cut the daily ration from three to two mugs.

The whole day big seas continued to sweep the boat without respite. The wilderness of foam and spray and white water seemed never ending. In the cabin everything was jumping, falling, flying. Glasses were smashed, a fire extinguisher broke loose; another torch went overboard. It was impossible to keep bottles upright even wedged in their pigeonhole and no food would stay on the table. Jam and sugar were spilled in the cupboards. It was again too rough to take any sights. The short end of the spinnaker-pole which we had wedged in the scuppers was lost overboard. It was of no immediate use but we had left the fittings on it and they could have been transferred to a new pole. My misery was increased by not being able to keep my sore hands dry. No plaster would stay on and a wet bandage was worse than none at all. Far from healing they were constantly painful, worse than when I had first done the damage. I was experiencing the literal meaning of the saying: 'To have salt rubbed into one's wounds.'

That evening at dusk the wind moderated a little, and the sea seemed slightly less. Jack pumped the bilges and again it took 200 strokes. Again we changed the storm jib for the working jib. Under this rig the sails were better balanced and we were able to set up the wind-vane self-steering. This was a big relief, for whoever was on watch had no need to stand at the tiller exposed to the full wind and sea, but could shelter in the lee of the cabin in the lower part of the cockpit, protected from wind and driven spray. With the self-steering we had an infinitely better night, though the log still kept fouling with blue strings of fish eggs. Our watches that night were, in order, Bob, Jack and me. By morning we were steering 140° compass, the wind had gone down to Force 4 or 5 and our speed was 4 to 6 knots. By the log we had run 145 miles since 1600 on day forty-five.

This was our forty-seventh day since Las Palmas. I got a morning sight (azimuth 94°) which put us in longitude 0° 45′ west. Unless we were becalmed we would cross the Greenwich meridian that evening. It was almost as much of a milestone as crossing the Equator. It seemed colder but perhaps it was because of wet clothes. In the morning the wind fell lighter again and we changed to the heavy genoa and shook the reefs out of the mainsail. This was our first chance to see the mainsail set full with the mended boom. At least it had stood up to the storm and now everything seemed strong enough. We had our first warm meal for some time: the familiar sausage rolls and a tin of beans. We started to dry our clothes and bedding.

In the last week when we changed head sails it was getting progressively harder to pull the wire halyard over its block at the masthead. From previous inspection I knew the sheave (the wheel of the pulley) was not turning, but I had hoped we could go on using it until we reached Cape Town. After all, though the halyard had been spliced, the splice didn't go through the block. However, when we changed to the genoa in the morning the sheave jammed immovably and we had to hoist the sail on the spinnaker halyard. In the afternoon the wind fell lighter again and the sea was down to a slow swell, so I decided to go up and have a look. I found the sheave, made of Tufnol, had been worn by the wire right down on one side, and the wire was jammed between the sheave and the cheek of the block. I got the wire free, but we weren't going to be able to use it and I didn't think we could change the block at sea. The block was fitted tightly in the angle of the forestay and the mast, the nut to unscrew it wasn't accessible without removing the forestay and though we had a spare block I wasn't sure we could bolt it on. Perhaps the spinnaker halyard, though it was rope, not wire, would do for the rest of the passage.

We made slower and slower progress as the day wore on. You might have thought that we would have welcomed a calm spell after a storm, but it shows the perversity of human nature that I found this almost as frustrating. In these days mountains of foreboding and gloom would settle on me, and my only means of escape was by meditation. Major breakdown, storms, calms – they all meant delay, day after day lost. I wondered not *when* we would get there, but *whether* we would get there. Hope deferred maketh the heart sick. I imagined water and provisions running short, more gear failing. I learned perhaps that for this kind of voyage the endurance needed is not only physical but mental. Patience and the ability to wait and suffer – or not to suffer! Of course the daily routine, the companionship, the little things, the beauty around us, were a constant antidote. My grey moods seldom lasted long and I tried not to show my depression to the others. As I have said, Jack also had his moods. Only Bob seemed to keep even-tempered and cheerful all through.

I shouldn't make too much of this. Indeed it is just as important to say that I got up to *Guardian* crossword number 15, we had beefburgers for lunch and an excellent stew for supper – a steak-and-kidney pudding with tinned vegetables and flour for thickening added. For dessert we had tinned pineapple and a piece of chocolate from my 'secret' store and last but not least a glass of wine.

I haven't said anything about sex in this chronicle because with no women on board and three heterosexuals, there wasn't any – only light banter and occasional after-dinner stories. We didn't let our hair down about our love-life and nobody seemed desperately frustrated. Thinking about it I fixed on three reasons why. First, sailing is all-absorbing and hard work. Mentally you have to keep an eye on everything and be constantly aware. Physically (quite apart from hauling ropes, handling sails, and maintenance) you are using every muscle in the body to balance, all day and part of the night. It's a tiring business.

The second reason is that you're never alone. Unlike the first reason, this applied as well during my four years in Japanese prison camp where the atmosphere was similar. With three or more, and sleeping close to your neighbours, you're leading a public life 24 hours a day. It might be different with a mixed couple who stay in port and spend all day in a double bunk.

The third reason is that all the stimuli of our sexy society cease to exist. At sea you don't see sexy adverts, come-hither dress fashions, passionate theatre, films or TV programmes. So we all seemed reasonably happy without. I expect Jack missed Heather, but the jokes he came out with were genuine enough. Once when Bob accidentally touched him on the shoulder be objected in a mincing treble: 'I know you fancy me, but it's no use. I'm not that kind of a boy.' Bob I'm sure had had affairs and when we got to Cape Town he charmed all the single girls and some of the married women as well. As for me, I was older than the other two and though the old song, 'folks go on to ninety-three, doing what comes naturally', is true enough, *anno domini* does calm things down a bit.

16

MORE TROUBLE

During the night we had no wind at all and the morning sight put us in longitude 0° 02′ east. We had just managed to crawl across the Greenwich meridian and the log showed a miserable day's run of 39 miles. All morning we were becalmed, and Bob proposed to go up the mast to see if he could do something about the jammed block. He was younger and stronger than I was, and I had respect for his ingenuity in devising *ad hoc* solutions to practical problems. So with the mainsail lowered we hauled him up on the 'bosun's chair' on the main halyard to have a look. He came down and went up again armed with a hacksaw, a spare block, an assortment of other tools and, in his head, various alternatives he proposed to try. Then when he reached the top and had started working, he somehow slipped off the bosun's chair. By the grace of God he didn't fall, but clung to the mast with the bosun's chair up round his shoulders.

It was a nasty situation. It was awkward enough to climb on to the swing seat on deck before being hauled up. At the top of the mast it would be doubly difficult. The chair now round his shoulders might be giving him some support, but it would take very little for it to slip over his head. He could not get it firmly under his bottom unless we slacked off on the halyard, and then he would have to use one hand to push and pull it into place, clinging to the mast meanwhile with his other hand. After exchanging shouted enquiries and instructions (luckily in the dead calm it was easy to hear), it was arranged we would slack off cautiously. Gradually and evidently with great effort, he was able to push the wooden seat down as we let go, until after what seemed an age, he was sitting on it once more. When he finally got down he was pale and shaking. 'I'll have a rest and give it another go' he said, but I persuaded him to give it up, supported in this by Jack. Bob was going to saw the old block out, and wasn't even sure he would be able to fix a new one. After all, we still had two halyards and could use the spinnaker halyard for all head sails. Having turned it end for end it was in good condition and there was no reason it shouldn't last out. I think we were all relieved, in fact, to have taken the easy way out, and there was a general relaxation after so much tension. That night for supper we had an excellent potato pie that Jack baked in the oven.

That evening when he was on watch Bob saw an orange-green flare to the west and we all turned out to have a look and speculate. The whole sky, it seemed, was lit up. We wondered if it was a distress signal but that should have been red. Perhaps it was a meteorite. Though we watched and waited, there was no repetition, and in any case there was not much we could have done.

The forty-ninth day we were in longitude 0° 49 west, 31° 14' south. We had long discussions (poring over the weather map and reading the Sailing Instructions) whether we should steer more to the south for better winds or direct for Cape Town by the shortest route. For the last few days we had been going due east, partly because of the storm from the south, and now we turned farther south until we were almost on the same parallel as Cape Town. I doubt in the end if it made much difference. Unless we had gone another 100 miles south we had as much chance of getting wind in one place as in another. As for catching up we were hopelessly behind schedule. I had hoped to reach Cape Town by 15 October at the latest. It was now the 26th and we still had over 900 miles to go. We now had a more moderate following sea and the wind behind us, gradually increasing during the day until we were going along nicely at 5 to 6 knots. As always we ran with the centre-board up. We would put it half-way down (fifteen turns of the winch) for reaching, and when close on the wind, the full thirty turns down. Because the wire needed repositioning on its drum if we let the board too far down, I got into the habit of logging how many turns up or down we made. The weather was much fresher, indeed it seemed to us quite chilly. That night in Bob's watch at 1130, a ship passed to the north of us. It was the first ship we had seen for over a month.

The next day we were in 2° 27' east, 32° 32' south, and our daily run was 89 miles. The wind continued from the north-west and we ran before it under the main and the heavy genoa boomed out with a whisker-pole. All the time we had visits from sea birds flying round the boat, more numerous now, it seemed, than farther north. Before the tropics when we had been near the Cape Verde Islands we had two visits from land birds that rested on the boat. One was a kind of swallow with a forked tail who settled on the after rail, fluttered round inside the cabin and later sat on the cabin top. It seemed sick and exhausted but would not eat or drink or let us get near. It disappeared in the night. The next day two tiny birds, no bigger than sparrows, came together, flew round the mast and perched on the rail near the bow. They were dark and spruce and seemed lively and well. Again they wouldn't take food or drink or make friends, and flew off after an hour or two.

Two weeks later when we were in 22° 40′ west and 1° 30′ north, a young sea bird, dark coloured, most likely a species of storm petrel, came on board. We noticed it first with others of its kind flying round the boat, but having trouble landing and taking off. It was during the tropical downpours and though it sat for a time near the bow, it later came into the cockpit and took shelter from the rain. It got in under the coaming, on a seat next to the life-raft and stayed there for the rest of that day and all night. In the morning it was still there but hadn't touched the water or biscuit we put beside it. Jack reckoned it had a damaged tail feather. It stayed until lunch time then flew away. Visits from birds on board are cheering as a sign of life but at the same time sad, because they are usually sick or exhausted and you can rarely help them.

The birds now flying round the boat included the biggest and strongest of any at sea, for we had several visits from the wandering albatross (*Diomeda exulans*) whose wing-span goes up to 11 feet, the largest among living birds. They came only occasionally and to me, apart from their size, were distinguished by the fact that they never moved their enormous wings. A smaller albatross, what Jack called a Cape albatross, would plane motionless for long periods but then, to gain height or direction, would give one or two beats. I never saw the big albatross make a single movement. Another feature (unlike the soft grace of many birds) was the bony angularity of their wings and bodies, giving an impression of immense power, almost of harshness. At all events they were a joy to watch. Here were we labouring along at 5 or 6 knots, and these heavenly creatures were soaring through the air at 50 to 70 miles an hour.

The fifty-first day we were in longitude 4° 10′ east, latitude 33° 46′ south. We still had another 750 miles to reach Cape Town. In the morning the following wind got up and there was another big sea with white horses and streaks of foam. We ran on all day under full main and genoa, slightly on the port tack with the wind on the port quarter, steering 120° with 24° of west variation. Sometimes it was hard work at the tiller holding the boat straight, as she surged down the face of the great waves. During the morning a whale surfaced a few yards off the starboard bow. Fortunately it seemed to be alone. We altered course quickly to pass it and had no trouble.

But trouble was waiting for us! At about 2130 when Bob was at the helm in the dark, *Swingaway* without warning swung broadside on and became unmanageable. I came out from the cabin with the sails as deafening as an artillery barrage, and found Bob swinging the tiller backwards and forwards as if it was the handle of a pump.

'Something's happened,' he shouted.

With a torch we gazed over the stern and as the counter rose and fell in the mountains and valleys of the sea, I looked with shocked unbelief at the rudder – or I should say at half the rudder. For about the waterline, where the metal part of the rudder ended and the two-inch thick wooden blade began, it had simply broken off, and all that was left was a line of splintered wood. By now Jack had come on deck too. All three of us gazed at the damage without a word.

The rudder was a complex structure of wood and metal, designed to be raised and lowered by a worm gear. To get enough grip on the water and provide adequate control and steerage, it went well below the main hull when lowered, but it could be lifted if the boat was in shallow water or beached. It was hung on the counter fixed by eyes to two stainless-steel plates which were bolted to the GRP hull. A single stainless-steel pin ran right down through the eyes on the rudder and the eyes on the counter. The whole thing was heavily built and extremely strong.

Traditional yacht design has in the past used a rudder held to the keel, or to the hull, or to a skeg, both at the top *and the bottom*. If part of the rudder is free in the water and projecting below the hull and keel, it cannot be so strongly held and will be subject to greater strains the more the keel is cut away. This is a feature of modern design not only in multihulls but also in monohulls. It may make for a faster boat, but there seems little doubt it could be a contributory cause of the rudder failures which do occur with modern designs – monohull as well as multihull. I have no idea in this case whether the rudder went suddenly or whether there was a gradual weakening. In either event we could have done little to avoid it. In the other rudder failure we heard about in Las Palmas it was the metal superstructure that broke. It seems there will be intolerable strains, something will go, but it depends on the individual unit which part. It is not that there was a weakness in the construction; it was being asked to do too much.

Our stunned contemplation lasted only seconds because the elements don't observe any truce. We rushed as a team to get the sails down, but not before the wind had torn another batten pocket in the main and we had lost another batten overboard. We got out the spare rudder. It was stowed under a mattress in one of the forward bunks. Not a replica of the original rudder, it was a flat, shaped piece of wood without any provision for raising or lowering. There was a socket at its head for the tiller and, separately stowed, there were two galvanised-iron shoulder-pieces with eyes projecting. These were to be bolted on to the wood to hang the rudder on the transom. It was lighter than the broken rudder, but even so it must have weighed a hundredweight. As I looked at it in the cockpit and looked at the heaving waves I was full of misgiving. Were we going to be able to fix it?

There was nothing more we could do that night, so we turned in. Again *Swingaway* lay comfortably ahull. The broken rudder was still on the stern but lashed down to prevent it moving about. I lay awake in my bunk, my mind too concentrated on the next day to let me sleep, and it was a relief when the dawn came. After breakfast we got going. Nobody hurried because I think we all felt that, in this sea, it was going to be difficult. By lunch-time we had the spare rudder fitted together and the broken rudder off and lashed down on deck forward of the mast. Everything was cleared away aft and we were ready to try. It was a measure of the seriousness of the problem that no one actually put any fears into words. We were all just unusually subdued.

Our first attempts were completely unsuccessful. It was easy enough to fit the two top eyes together and push the long stainless steel pin through; it was the bottom fixing that was difficult. To start with it was right under water. We could only reach it by hanging upside down, head under water with a second person at the stern holding our heels. We couldn't use the snorkel at this angle and it meant holding one's breath and working a few seconds at a time. The plunging of the boat made it no easier for at one moment the stern would be two feet under the water, the next two feet in the air. Then the rudder had to go right down into the water but being entirely of wood it tended to float, and pushing it down was like trying to sink an air-filled balloon. Trying to hold it steady from the top proved hopeless. Bob tried getting into the water but there was no purchase and it was impossible to do anything.

The rudder itself was a constant menace, plunging this way and that, threatening to knock or crush our fingers, breaking away. After about an hour I got my hand caught and my thumb cut to the bone. There was blood everywhere and, suffering from shock, I turned pale and dizzy. I was never very good with blood. Once as an apprentice air-raid warden I fainted in a lecture because our instructress (a formidable woman) kept repeating the word – blood . . . blood . . . blood . . . blood – Jack took charge of me, covered me up in my bunk and dosed me with cups of hot, sweet tea.

'This is what you need,' he said.

What with the skin off my fingers which hadn't healed yet, my hands were a mess, and from then on, once I had steadied myself and come on deck again, I had to leave the main work to Jack and Bob, though I held tools or ropes or other people's heels, as required. Our next idea was to get a rope round the blade of the rudder and lead it round the stern to cleats in the cockpit. This was a big advance as it held the rudder much more firmly. We then tried lashing the eyes, to hold them together until we could push the main pin down, but the lashings failed to hold the eyes in a true enough line. Then we tried temporary pins (using short bolts) to fix the bottom and then the top eyes separately. These pins we pushed up from below, the plan being that the main pin coming down from above would push them out as it went in. This was almost successful, but in the end we lost our only bolts without getting the rudder on. At the same time several tools went overboard. (We hadn't learned our lesson from the last time thoroughly enough and in our anxiety had omitted to tie them on to a line.) More than six times (each involving long, careful preparation, heavy muscular effort, and somebody working under water) we nearly got the pin through the holes in the rudder and the stern. Six times, often at the last moment, the sea tore the rudder away and we were back where we started.

We had been working on this all day and were nearly all-in. Darkness was coming on. Now we were alarmed to see that the top eye fixed in the stern had started moving and twisting in the fibreglass of the hull. We had no fibreglass repair kit, and if we damaged the hull so it would not hold the rudder firmly, then our spare rudder was not going to be much use to us. I had the unhappy conviction that at sea, once damage to the fibreglass started it would steadily get worse, and a little play would lead to more and more damage. By then Jack and Bob were exhausted and could do no more. We finished the day worse off in every way than when we started. However, we went below and had a drink and sat and discussed what our prospects were if it came to the worst, that is if we couldn't get the rudder fitted.

We were 700 miles from Cape Town and also from the nearest shipping lane, which went up the coast. *Swingaway* almost certainly couldn't be kept on a course, even before the wind, without a rudder and the alternative was drifting as we were at an estimated half-a-knot east and north, say 12 miles a day. We had water for thirty days at our present ration of two mugs and food for perhaps fifty days. It would take us sixty days to drift near the shipping lane, though that might not hold if the wind was contrary. In any case with a reduced water ration that left us ten days in which to die of hunger or thirst. On the other hand we might get some rain, and there was some liquid in the tinned food. The range of our Sea-Link transmitter was optimistically 50 to 80 miles, the range of our rockets 5 to 6 miles by night, and our smoke flares by day 3 miles. Neither the life raft nor dinghy would be any improvement on staying with the yacht. We would hoist a radar reflector and a visual SOS — a square flag and a ball.

'Then it's best to stay in bed,' said Jack. 'You use the least energy and keep warm.'

It was a gloomy discussion, but I think it did us all good to talk about it. I'm not sure that any of us really believed deep down that somehow we wouldn't get out of it. Although things were, if anything, worse than the previous evening, I turned in and slept well instead of lying awake.

God knows how I would have felt if I had been alone. I had sailed single-handed across the North Sea, but nothing had gone wrong — I was in home waters then and there was the likelihood of help from other boats in the area. Being with other people, if they are good and don't panic, they encourage you and, encouraged, you support and sustain them in turn. I was lucky with both Jack and Bob. They stayed calm and positive throughout the crisis.

The next day, our fifty-fourth from Las Palmas, there was a cold south-west wind and the sea seemed as big or bigger than ever. The barometer showed 1031 millibars rising, the temperature was down to 60° Fahrenheit, and a morning sight put us 6° 01′ east. The previous day's morning sight had given me 5° 39′ east so it seemed we had drifted 22 miles in twenty-four hours, faster than we had reckoned the previous evening. But then there would be calm days. We all seemed in better form and better spirits than the previous evening. The first thing to do was to examine the hull where the rudder fitting was twisting and this meant crawling aft behind the engine. When we unbolted it, we found the fibreglass of the hull firm and undamaged, as strong and good as new, and reassuringly thick. What had happened was that when the boat was built, the holes for the rudder fitting had been drilled half-an-inch out of place, then two other correctly-placed holes were drilled alongside, making together a sort of figure of eight. Since there was room for play, the bolts had moved with the pulling and pushing. We were able to readjust them, put in wedges to stop any play and screw the fitting tighter than before.

The next thing we did was to move everything movable in the boat as far into the bows as we possibly could. Water, fuel, life-raft, gratings, floor boards, tools, tins of food, cooking pots, bottles, gas containers, radios, cushions, bedding, batteries, sails, ropes, wind-vane, wind generator, table, books, cutlery, paint, oil – everything. Gradually the forward cabin got more and more crammed until it was hardly possible to wedge the last few items in. Gradually the bow sank into the water and the stern rose. This was Jack's idea and it was of vital importance. Then we got three ropes on the rudder to hold it more firmly – one to the head of the rudder from the stern railing, one in the middle holding it hard to one side, and one right round the blade, pulling it the other way against the second rope. Then to replace the temporary bolts that had gone to the bottom of the ocean, we cut up a metal outboard bracket from the rubber dinghy and made pins to hold the rudder *pro tem*. Then we had a long rest and a good lunch of steak-and-kidney and carrots. After lunch Bob and Jack set to work still with heels in the air and head at times in the water, but not plunging so deeply because of the weight in the bow. By now too the sea was not quite so bad. First they got the two temporary pins in place. Then Bob gradually pushed down the main pin, and Jack, while I held his heels, guided it into place under water. Finally he rose dripping and breathless, and announced – 'It's home!'

Once again we had a rudder swinging at the stern. By 1630 we were under way. It was a moment of triumph. We all felt more jubilant and excited by our success than if we had never had any trouble with the rudder at all. Once we had restored order below decks Bob made three outsize mugs of tea and we raised them in a toast 'To Cape Town!'

17

Journey's End

That evening, to celebrate, we had a grand dinner – roast pork with gravy, peas and potatoes, with peaches to follow and the second-last bottle of our duty-free champagne. By the next day with the wind still cold and blowing west-south-west we had covered 70 miles and by noon were in latitude 34° 07′ south, longitude 7° 35′ east. The rudder was performing satisfactorily, it seemed well balanced and steered easily though with a slight shuddering. For some reason I never discovered, it was more difficult to set up any self-steering, and from then on one of us had to be always at the helm.

I spent the morning sewing my sleeping bag which had split down the side (I wish they would make them wider) and had a shave. During the voyage I shaved every two or three days, while Jack and Bob both grew realistic-looking beards. To begin with I used part of my precious fresh-water ration, but soon gave up such waste and found that shaving-soap lathered pretty well in hot salt water, though previously I have found salt-water soap poor stuff. I used to heat the water in the kettle, but on one occasion forgot to pour out what was left, and when we came to make a cup of tea, the result was unpopular to say the least. Thereafter, following trenchant comments from the others, I was careful to use one of the saucepans. The bandage on my thumb was good and firm so I left it on. Now the storm had abated I could keep my hands dry, and my fingers and palms were beginning to heal.

That night the wind got up again. To play safe, what with the boom and rudder both vulnerable, we lowered the main and ran under heavy genoa alone. At first our speed dropped to 3 or 4 knots but during the night it increased again from 4 to 6 knots. As always with strong enough wind, the sounds of the sea were accompanied by the howl of the wind generator. The next morning, with the wind more southerly, there was a lumpy sea on the beam and ahead. We were going with an uncomfortable motion, sometimes bumping hard and doing 4 to 6 knots under the genoa alone.

For breakfast Bob and Jack had spaghetti as a starter but I stuck to biscuits, marge and treacle with my coffee. We were down to our last pack of margarine and our last tin of treacle. The marmalade was all finished. Our fresh food had gone long ago, even potatoes. We had also got through the lemon juice but we were taking vitamin tablets. When we got going again after breaking the rudder we decided by a majority of two to one (Jack was against) to increase the water ration from two to three mugs a day. After all we were then in 9° 36′ east and we were suffering more and more from dehydration.

After breakfast we hoisted the mainsail and went on with an easier motion, still on a reach and steering 120° magnetic. The noon sight gave 34° 02′ south which was farther north than I had expected, but it was probably due to a northerly current. In the afternoon the wind backed to the south-east and we were close hauled at 3 to 5 knots. In the morning we had tried to run the engine. What with one thing and another we had left it for a week and it proved too much for the batteries. The ignition light was completely dead and we couldn't get it going. At this stage it was not vital to our progress, but it might make it difficult going into a strange port, and after the way we had nursed it and worked on it, it was disappointing to have it go, and added to the already long list of gear failures. Bob pumped the bilges again and after some days it took only 120 strokes to clear them.

We had a bad night for progress. The wind gusted in the evening so we reefed the mainsail and changed from the genoa to the working jib. It turned out to be the wrong decision, since the wind fell lighter and lighter in the night. We were on the starboard tack, steering between 110° and 130° compass as the wind varied. It was too cloudy to get a morning sight, but later simultaneous sights of sun and moon gave 11° 45′ east, 33° 34′ south. In the morning Bob got a radio bearing on Cape Town which must have been 350 miles away. Allowing half convergency it was a true bearing of approximately 90° degrees. It was our fifty-sixth day from Las Palmas. Later in the radio news from Cape Town, the announcer puzzled us when he referred to a match in the MCC's tour. The match in Cape Town had been delayed, he said, because of snow. We thought that Cape Town was too warm for snow particularly in November. It was only much later we realised Snow was the name of England's fast bowler!

All that morning we were almost becalmed but the wind came again from the south in the afternoon and reached Force 4.

That evening we wondered again whether we should play safe and reduce sail. The weather seemed settled and we had seen a perfect rainbow to the north stretching without a break from side to side of the horizon – a very satisfying sight, turning our thoughts to crocks of gold and the like. On a smaller scale there had been earlier occasions when spray from the floats would fly up into the sun and *Swingaway* would race along creating her own private rainbow. Another indication was that there were sea birds still flying round the boat as it got dark, and one settled peacefully on the water. My experience is that if there is going to be a serious blow, they get out of the way. So we carried on under full sail, the wind stayed light with stars in the sky and we made fair progress.

These last days before Cape Town were wearisome. Many of our supplies were running short. There was no let up from the constant motion, the salt air, the damp and now the cold. There was dirt everywhere and it was more and more difficult to wash clothes, dishes or ourselves. There was no let up from night watches nor, with the jury rudder, from tricks at the helm. To add to everything our electricity was failing. The wind generator was not charging enough even to light the compass let alone the navigation lights. We were thrown back on the Tilley lamp and torches.

Our run the next day was 96 miles. The wind veered to the west and we ran under main and heavy genoa, the two sails goose-winged. In the afternoon the wind veered to the north and we carried on at about 5 knots steering 110°. In the evening the wind was strong, and with no compass light, we decided to lower the sails and lie ahull for the night. It was warm in the cabin and we all slept well. By morning the wind was blowing hard from the south, about Force 7, and we got under way under jib alone, hoisting the mainsail later as the wind fell slightly. That evening we were surrounded by an enormous school of porpoises, plunging a dozen at a time across the bows. There were flocks of birds diving into the water too, so there must have been a big shoal of fish to attract them all. Nobody thought of fishing and probably we were going too fast to have put a line out. For lunch we had beans and for supper steak-and-kidney pie, carrots and dried mashed potato. The wine was finished.

We passed a ship in the night at 0130 in Bob's watch, going from east to west. In the morning (our sixtieth day and 5 November) there was light following wind and we hoisted the spinnaker after breakfast. An indication of how inefficient we were getting and how badly we needed a break, was that three times we made a mess of hoisting it. Once we got the whole sail under the stern and foul of the rudder and propeller. Fortunately it was undamaged and finally we got it properly set. A morning sight made our longitude 16° 56′ east which gave us 70 miles to go to Cape Town. All morning we carried the spinnaker, steering first on the starboard then on the port tack and took it down at 1300.

We were under main and genoa steering 100° magnetic, when I saw land ahead. It was the high outline of Table Mountain quite unmistakable and 30 to 40 miles distant. It was 1600 hours, we were doing 4 knots with a following breeze, so another ten hours would see us in under the land. As we spliced the mainbrace and made double cups of tea, we discussed whether we should carry on after Cape Town.

'Pack it in,' suggested Bob. He'd had enough of the sea for a while.

I concurred. It seemed the best thing to do. I had promised to be back in England by January and it might take another three months to get everything fixed and reach Australia let alone New Zealand. Jack seemed non-committal, saying very little, but made no objection. Of course we would all have to wait and see. Jack and Bob would have to get jobs in South Africa, and in Bob's case, go on eventually to New Zealand, and I would have to do something about the boat.

18

AT THE CAPE

Jack had the first watch and when I came up at 0100 to take over it seemed as if we could have reached out and touched the lights of the city just ahead. With no engine and the wind light from the west I didn't want to get on a lee shore, so before Jack turned in we got the sails down and lay ahull for the rest of the night. In the morning Table Mountain was lost in the clouds, there was drizzling rain and we were about three-quarters of a mile off shore, looking at rocks, surf breaking on a bathing beach, and behind what looked like beach hotels and suburban houses perching on the slopes. As usual on a strange coast (and off our large-scale chart of Table Bay) it wasn't easy to tell exactly where we were – later we found it was Camps Bay. We had picked up Roben Island light during the night and our way evidently lay north. We had to tack along the coast and it was 0930 before we rounded the end of the harbour breakwater, getting an unofficial welcome from a solemn seal who came to the surface near a beacon and stayed with his head out looking placidly at us. It was a delightful moment. For me his wise look was also a friendly farewell from the creatures of the sea.

The light wind from the north-west was the best we could have had for finding our way into the yacht harbour without an engine, and under jib alone we glided gently through two basins for liners and cargo-boats until we saw the usual cluster of masts. Once inside things were more crowded and we tied up to a buoy near the entrance. A coloured 'boy' in a launch caught a line and took us ashore to the Royal Cape Yacht Club where we got the friendliest of welcomes. Though the staff were heavily engaged with the many big yachts in a Whitbread Round-the-World Race, they had time for us. Soon *Swingaway* was moored alongside a wooden landing-stage not 30 yards from the Yacht Club. It was Thursday when we arrived and the place was buzzing with life, as the yachts in the race were to set off the next day for Sydney. A centre had been set up near the

Club with a mobile post-office, bank, shop and cafeteria. The Club itself was crowded with racing crews, friends and helpers. We cleared customs, immigration and health authorities in the morning and they stamped our passports with visitors' permits. We had beer in the Yacht Club and chicken à la king in the cafeteria.

After lunch I went into town by a temporary bus service. It was another of the facilities arranged for the race. It was a long walk from the Club to town and, as we found later after some weary journeys, there was no public transport. I wandered through the centre of Cape Town with its great buildings, squares, gardens, and excellent shops. Apartheid was not as universal as I had supposed. It applied in the official world (post-office, railway station, government departments) but less in the commercial world (shops, restaurants, banks). The unacceptable aspects were less obvious to the casual observer and in any case we were in the most liberal part of the country. Cape newspapers were freely critical. All the same, among the people who entertained us Africans seemed not to exist, except as servants. There were separate non-white suburbs. The cinema was all white. On the long journey to Johannesburg the train had far more black passengers and only four black carriages to nine white. A pathetic sight we noticed, being near the docks, was of black manual dock-workers arriving in the morning dressed in city-suits carrying brief-cases. No doubt many things have changed now.

I called and picked up some letters then went on to a big store where I bought fresh meat, cheese, coffee, milk, wine. Then I went to the market for fresh vegetables and fruit. After so long at sea the colour and bustle of the market and the town generally were like a vision, a luminous medley of sights and sounds and scents. I stopped at one of the many fruit-juice bars offering chilled apple, peach, orange, guava, pomegranate or grape juice. After a glass of peach juice – luxury for a salt-saturated palate – I got the bus back to the harbour. That night we dined on *escalope de veau* with a green salad, asparagus, melon, coffee with *fresh milk* and our last bottle of champagne.

In the next few days I got in touch with a firm for the engine who would also charge the batteries, a sail-maker, a welder for the boom, a wood-worker who would replace the rudder, a yacht-broker. I wrote to England for a new boom, an outline drawing of the rudder, and a new wind-gauge. Before the week was out Jack had got himself a job. It was third mate on a fisheries research vessel working for the University, which went out a week or so at a time. They would pay him 250 Rand a month (about £200) and he would get free board, lodging and laundry. He moved his gear off *Swingaway* and we only saw him again when he visited us from time to time. I had an argument with him on one of his early visits. He still wanted to go on to New Zealand and blamed me for ending the cruise at Cape Town. Though he had his good job he was worried about the immigration authorities (who hadn't given us work permits) and also because he hadn't heard from his wife, Heather. Ironically a factor in ending the cruise was my reluctance (and Bob's) to make another long passage with him. His signalling expertise was more suited to a big ship and his vital work on the rudder and his keenness at other times were balanced by his temperamental outbursts, latterly more frequent.

In the last day before we reached Cape Town there had been two occasions. When I saw the outline of Table Mountain ahead of us and enthusiastically announced it to the others, Jack's response was: 'Oh that. I saw it two hours ago.'

Whether he was just boasting or whether he had seen the long-awaited landfall and not told us – but why, when we had been living for that moment? – I don't know. Again that same night, when I came up at 0100 to take over the watch, his last remark before going below had been: 'If you wake me up unnecessarily before morning I'll give you a black eye.'

Childishly but at least cheerfully I retorted: 'Then I'll give you one back.'

'I was only joking,' said Jack.

These were strange remarks when we were in sight of our goal, and the more so as (owing to the sequence of watches) I had never woken Jack at night either for regular watch or in emergency. If he had come on deck he had done so voluntarily. I thought no more at the time of these incidents for I was delighted to have arrived. Maybe Jack, uncertain of his future plans, had felt secure on board, and didn't want the cruise to end.

I think in retrospect I can understand better. We had our problems on the voyage, but we had escaped completely from other problems. It was a simple, straightforward kind of life with only one aim: to get the ship there as safely, as easily and as quickly as possible. By contrast, think of the bewildering paraphernalia of modern existence, the pressures both objective and subjective: commuting, cars, television, permits, licences, bank-accounts, junk-mail, traffic wardens, relatives, guests, appointments, telephones, holidays, airports, appeals, credit-cards, keys, shopping, money, housework, gardening, bills, dinner-parties, doctors' appointments, anniversaries, the problem of presents, jobs, redundancies, negotiations, crime, decisions to be taken – decisions, decisions, decisions. Many people want as little of this as possible and maybe Jack, who'd led a Navy life from thirteen or fourteen years old, wanted less than most. There could be a real attraction in having it all decided for you.

Bob and I went on living aboard *Swingaway*. Bob was not so lucky with a job, though he applied for several and got one selling an educational encyclopaedia door-to-door. Unfortunately this was on commission and meant working for nothing since he didn't sell a single one. He could have got a free air-ticket to Hong Kong to navigate a new yacht from Hong Kong to the Seychelles, but there were some details he wasn't sure about and he turned it down. We had a comfortable berth in the harbour and from first to last the Club people could not have been more helpful. But there was one big drawback – coal. Tons of coal were shipped out through the port and to handle this and other cargo a fleet of locomotives, old-fashioned steam-engines, went huffing and puffing through the night even at week-ends. This made sleep fitful and in addition the Cape 'doctor', the local name for the south-east Trades, now well set in, spread a permanent layer of coal-dust and grit over the deck and the cockpit.

The best part of these weeks was climbing on Table Mountain and excursions to places near-by. The enormous mass of Table Mountain dominates not only Cape Town, but the country for miles around. Rising 3500 feet direct from sea-level, it is just as impressive as far higher peaks surrounded by highlands. The Saturday after we arrived Bob proposed a climb to the top. He had been to the local tourist office and I thought knew all about it. We took a bus to Kloof Nek, the col between Table Mountain and Lion's Head where the road runs round Cape Peninsula, and walked along a side road past the cable-car and through a giant shadow cast by the sun. Bob had been told the easiest route was up the Patteclip Gorge turning off the road past the cable-car. We had no map, we were lightly clad and had no proper boots. We had some bread, sardines and fruit to eat.

We identified the Gorge all right, a rocky gulley that ran straight up from the road with a well-defined path. After a few hundred yards the path seemed to lead off to the east along the side of the mountain. As we climbed the sun disappeared and the clouds came down lower and lower. In an hour or so we were completely lost, now climbing on more and more precipitous cliff faces, now struggling through thick shrubs and high grass. Once we lost each other in the mist and drizzle and only came together after a lot of shouting. Our clothes and feet were sodden and it was quite cold. We kept going but I doubt if we would have got to the top. I'm not sure we would have got down either before daylight the next day, for there were some rock faces we had been able to get up, but couldn't have got down. Then going along a ledge with overhanging rock above and a drop below (how far we couldn't see for the mist) we came on two climbers sheltering from the drizzle in a niche.

We couldn't have fallen into better hands. We introduced ourselves and Alan and Vernon told us we had followed a contour path right round to the other side of the mountain to the Ledges, where there are some stiff rock-climbing routes to the summit. It would have been ironic to have come to grief on the mountain after surviving our voyage! They led us to the top, past one difficult bit, almost a jump across, that we wouldn't even have tried on our own. There we lit a fire and had some lunch. Then we tramped across the broad top of the Table to the summit restaurant for tea and toast, went down in the cable-car and they gave us a lift back to the boat.

They came to tea on the boat the next day, Sunday, with their wives, Jeanne and Alta, and we became almost part of the family. Bob was a universal favourite and being so good with kids was a welcome addition to families everywhere. They took us climbing or walking nearly every week-end, not only all over Table Mountain, but to Stellenbosch, to the Kleine Drakensberg and to the Bains Kloof Forest Reserve. At Bains Kloof, thanks to them and to a permit for the Reserve, I had four days away from the boat, walking and climbing with the world to myself. This time I did have a map. It was dry, hot weather, I slept under the stars, climbed three peaks over 5000 feet, and walked and swam in lonely river-valleys, with one great waterfall plunging some 500 feet to a deep mysterious pool. Besides birds and insects the only living things I saw were rock rabbits, mountain deer and some kind of African wild cat, quite sizable, which, I'm glad to say, bounded past me a few yards off while I was having lunch.

We also had a splendid day when Jeanne lent us her car and Bob and I drove 38 miles round Cape Peninsula where the mountains meet the sea in mile on mile of dazzling beaches, rocky headlands, wooded valleys, cloud-capped peaks – as rich a concentration of dramatic scenery as anywhere in the world. Near the lighthouse at the far end of Africa, we had a coldish swim off a steep beach, a suspicious group of cormorants watching us. As we were leaving, a Cape baboon jumped on the bonnet and scolded us through the windscreen.

Much of the country round Cape Town is a land of rock and stone where the bones stick out, yellow, brown, slate grey. A country without the rich flesh of meadows, an anatomy of skin and bone. There are jagged outcrops, antique weathered pillars, sheer heights, smooth slopes, polished faces. From mountainsides to great boulders, to small pebbles, everywhere is rock. Ground down, it blows in the winds, drifts in the hills and valleys, forms dry river-beds, inland sand-dunes, sea-less beaches. There are stony rivers, gritty paths, strong winds, dust and beating sun. Some slopes are thinly clad in low scrub with glossy leaves and strange shapes. Elsewhere the land is studded with a never-ending variety of vivid wild flowers with mysterious names – Protea, Wilsonia, Chincherinchee, Agapanthus, Leguminosae, Scabiosa, Potentilla. There are pink 'painted-ladies', deep-blue irises, bright scarlet ice-plant and blood-red lichens – clear, strong, gem-like colours.

The weather is harsh, uncompromising too, not like the soft melancholy of Britain. The Trade winds were now established and they blew stronger and stronger. From then on I never saw the sea without white caps.

'Damn good thing we got here before this started,' Bob remarked.

The dust and beating sun would change when the wind brought cloud that sometimes poured over the edge of Table Mountain like a ghostly waterfall. To the locals it was 'the table-cloth' for their flat-topped peak.

In the yacht harbour we met a number of the round-the-world brigade. It seems there is a constant trickle of yachts coasting from port to port with a minimum of long hops, and often spending much longer in port than at sea. The 'milk-run' as some call it goes from east to west – across the Indian Ocean, round the African coast, across to the West Indies and on to the South Seas. They include a number of shoe-string sailors and some, with clapped-out boats, few charts and poor equipment, get only a short way. Some will stay in port living cheaply on board for months or even years. To encourage them to move on the Royal Cape Club had fixed dues that increased as time elapsed. Moorings and membership were free for two months, then they charged £10 a month, increasing to about £50 after a year.

One Australian couple, Fred and Milly, had been there for nearly twelve months. Fred was a welder by trade, he had built his own boat, a 35-foot steel ketch, in Perth and sailed from there with his girl-friend. They invited us for supper and gave us a conducted tour of the boat. If not the most elegant of yachts, she was strong and comfortable and had sailed well on the crossing to Africa. He had no trouble earning a living from casual jobs around the port without being bothered by the authorities, but now they were getting ready to go on up the coast. Dick and Sadie were a less well-organised couple who arrived when we were there. Dick was a huge blond always on the look-out for cast-off rope or other gear for his boat; Sadie was a rather unhappy, unkempt girl with a baby who never stopped crying. On a small boat it must have been nerve-racking. They had come from Nairobi and their boat was all bits and pieces – mast at an angle, hull patched, paint peeling. Even granted that Dick was as strong as a horse, I wondered how they had made it. They all came along for supper one evening and as time wore on, the party (encouraged by Bob) got noisier. They would have settled down to an all-night drinking session, except that half the guests were sitting on my bunk, and through sheer weariness I had to kick them out at half-past-midnight in order to turn in. An even more exotic visitor was a young Japanese who came in a few days before we left, having sailed single-handed from Japan round the Horn.

It wasn't all socialising and holiday ashore. Gradually with help from Bob and local firms I got the list of lost, broken or damaged items made good. We slipped the boat and painted the bottom. I wrote endless letters, sent telegrams and even telephoned suppliers in England. More and more time went by. Eventually I had an offer for the boat. It was from a television dealer who had shipped in, I don't know – thousands of sets from Germany, anticipating the first TV transmissions to come to Cape Town and was potentially in the money. He came down to the boat, a smart young man, with a bevy of play-boys and dolly-girls who could have gone on the set of a soap opera. He had never sailed in his life, but he fancied the look of *Swingaway* and money was no object. He would pay me in Swiss francs, German marks, pounds sterling – gold bars I expect, if I'd wanted them. We invited them for lunch and we sat and drank to the sale while Bob fed us on *boerswors*, a local spiced sausage, and coffee. Alas – when Fridjohn, the broker, rang our buyer later it appeared he didn't have the money after all.

Then came an offer from Durban, something more serious this time. Ron Senogles had already sailed a Piver tri, and was actually looking for an Ocean Bird. He flew down from Durban, fell in love with *Swingaway* and we settled the deal the same day over lunch in the Yacht Club. I would get almost what the yacht had cost me but not allowing for nearly £1000 spent in Cape Town. Ron would take the boat over where she was and bring a crew down to sail her up the coast to Durban.

I also had a last argument with Jack which followed the pattern of the others: confrontation then agreement. He came along one day and told me he had been discussing his situation and, as captain, I was responsible for his passage to New Zealand. The sale of the boat was not then quite finalised, Jack and I had settled accounts, and I wasn't prepared for this. I had an appointment the same day with Fridjohn, the broker, who was also a qualified lawyer, so I asked Jack to come back later. Fridjohn laughed when I told him about it.

'He's got no legal claim on you at all,' he said. 'He's not your hired crew and there's no contract to that effect. You made a friendly arrangement to sail here and if you've shared expenses he's no more claim on you than you have on him.'

When Jack came back I passed this on to him and he took it like a lamb. In fact he was half apologetic.

Taking a chance on the sale (and a deep breath) I felt an obligation to 'do the decent thing' and decided to refund Jack's (modest) contribution to the boat and see he had enough for a flight to the UK, which would at least satisfy the immigration authorities. He was then even more amiable and insisted on giving me a conducted tour over the fisheries research vessel where he was working – and very interesting it was. We parted with handshakes and mutual good wishes. I told Bob what had happened and offered him the same, but he wouldn't accept.

'I'll be all right,' he said. 'I'm getting some dough from New Zealand. It was a great experience.'

Then it was farewell to South Africa. Ron Senogles arrived with his crew. I said goodbye and gave presents to the staff at the Yacht Club, spent a night in a bed-and-breakfast place in town and took the train the next day for the long journey to Johannesburg. After

Cape Town Johannesburg seemed featureless and unattractive, but I only had time to wander round the centre and get a night's sleep.

Leaving at noon, the Boeing 707 touched down at Mauritius on Christmas Eve, and reached a windy aerodrome near Perth in Western Australia at sunrise. After Melbourne I had roast turkey and plum pudding in the air courtesy of Quantas and arrived at Sydney on Christmas afternoon. After four days with friends, another few hours' flying saw me reunited with my sister in Wellington, New Zealand. The air trip had taken about 30 hours in all. In *Swingaway* it would have been more interesting, but it would have taken a little longer.

Epilogue
Tying Rope-Ends

What happened to the characters in the tale I've been describing? The most important character, the boat, will have a long and honourable career. She was to have a good home and an experienced owner. She would spend her days cruising in the waters round Durban and, as Ron intended, taking part in the annual Durban to Lourenço Marques Race. My accounts of breakages and damage might be taken as criticism of design or structure. But in reality she was a beauty – good to live in and exciting to sail. When I looked round the cabin on leaving, it was as comfortable and livable in as the day I'd first seen her in Lymington. Perhaps she had been too much of a thoroughbred for such long, hard work. Perhaps we amateurs should have had a dull plod on a cart-horse. But her design and finish were a tribute to West Country craftsmanship. The scars had come partly from our clumsy handling, partly from pushing her too hard in the endless struggle against the sea which is the life of every boat.

I had at least learned *that* in our long voyage. Every minute the wind and sea are looking for weakness: to wear out sails, to chafe through rope, to rub away metal; to find cracks, chinks, hairlines; to leak in, to wet, to spoil, to corrode. In any fitting they find the weakest part, shake it, pull it, strain it again and again. Anything loose will be broken free, blown away, lost overboard. The struggle is never-ending and the elements never give up.

The second character, Jack, had settled into a job for which he was well-qualified and, having agreed with the authorities, could stay in South Africa or return to England as he pleased. He could even have gone on to New Zealand. In sum his contribution to the voyage had been as valuable as anyone's. Our disagreements had been storms in tea-cups and hadn't scarred either of us for life.

Bob's future is the sad part of this story. When I left he was staying ashore with a friend and flew back to New Zealand shortly after I did. He started school-teaching again in Temuka, a little town in the South Island. One afternoon he was returning home on a push-bike when he was killed in an accident. Two youngsters in cars were racing each other down the street and Bob didn't have a chance. *Lacrimae Rerum.* Is it the best of us who are killed? Sometimes during the war it seemed so. His parents came and called on me in London later, quiet, decent people who deserved better. He was a great chap and has left an unfillable gap in that circle of individuals who count as life-long friends whether they live in New Zealand or Patagonia.

I had a rewarding stay in New Zealand, mostly in Paraparaumu where my sister lived, and got back to London in reasonable time for the business of the cinema.

Before I left, a friend in Auckland arranged for me to go out with some others on a boat belonging to the Commodore of the Yacht Club and I was to be on the pier at eleven sharp. When I got there an anxious member of the crew greeted me:

'You haven't got the beer have you?'

It arrived shortly after – three cases of it. Then the rest of the crew turned up and I found they were all journalists on the *Auckland Herald*, all six of them. I was the only one who went in for a swim from the boat and I was evidently considered a little eccentric. I went in before what was a very liquid lunch, appropriately since we had sailed down the harbour and anchored in Drunkard's Bay – so called because sailing ships used to put in there to let the crew sober up before going out into the open sea. Journalists generally are good, solid beer-drinkers and so are New Zealanders – as Bob was on occasions. Fortunately I had got to know and respect his other qualities.

Appendix 1
Stores and Equipment Carried

I STORES

About £70 of tinned food (at 1970s prices) and £35 of fresh food (£20 from U.K., £15 from Las Palmas).

Tinned Food

Meat – Sausages, sausage rolls, bully beef, steak-and-kidney puddings, luncheon meat, tongue, chicken, sliced beef, pork, etc.

Fish – Sardines, herrings, salmon, mackerel, fish pastes.

Vegetables – Peas, carrots, tomatoes, green beans, haricot beans, baked beans, beetroot, spinach.

Fruit – Peaches, pears, plums, apricots, cherries, raspberries, blackcurrants, etc.

Miscellaneous – 5lbs marmalade, tins jam, syrup, honey, jar sweets. Margarine. Dried milk. Potato powder. Marmite (yeast extract). Packets of soup. Pickles. 10 tins waterbiscuits. Sweet biscuits. Oatmeal, lentils, flour.

Fresh Food

Meat – Chops, sausages, fresh chicken, ham, bacon. Cheese. Eggs. Fish, etc. Kippers.

Vegetables – Potatoes, turnips, swedes, carrots, parsnips, cabbages.

Fruit – Apples, bananas, melons, grapes, oranges.

Miscellaneous Provisions

Tea. Soluble coffee. Sauces. Pepper. Herbs. Loaves of bread.

We should have taken more fresh and tinned fruit as this is what one has most taste for. There was no desire for salty things or need to add salt in cooking.

Drink

About £25 of duty-free alcohol (whisky 40 pence a bottle), and 75 gallons of water.
One dozen mixed spirits – whisky, rum and gin.
Five dozen cans beer.
Two dozen bottles wine.

We should have taken more beer and wine and fewer bottles of spirits.

II   EQUIPMENT AND SPARES

In addition to the general equipment of the boat:

3 torches and plenty of dry batteries.
Supply of timber – assorted lengths and sizes of softwood.
Spare rope and twine.
Spare rigging wire, soft wire, electric wiring.
Nails, screws, washers, split pins, bolts and nuts.
Spare shackles, eyes, clamps, bulldog clips, etc.
Twine, thread, needles, sail needle and palm, scissors.
Paint, waterproof stopping, plastic padding.
Rubber hose and plastic tubing.
Set of spares for WC.
Engine spares – spark plugs, coil, gasket, etc.
Carpenter's tools – hammer, saw, plane, chisel, screwdrivers, auger, oilstone, lino knife, rule, etc.
Mechanic's tools – spanners, pliers, screwdrivers, wrench, hack-saw, etc.

Clothes, etc. – sleeping bag, pillow, towels, oilskins, anorak, jerseys, jeans, working shirts, gloves, sea boots, canvas shoes, woollen socks, underclothes, shore clothes.

Appendix 2
Technical Note

In this book there are naturally many words describing equipment, fittings, sailing, weather and so on. In case of need the reader should find them in a good general dictionary. Or if for any reason you can't or don't want to look them up, the story should be plain without a precise definition. Nevertheless the non-mathematical reader may appreciate a short explanation about one aspect of navigation.

Most people think of a journey in terms of: first right, second left, then its number 22; or after Birmingham turn left off the M6 on to the A5 and follow it to Holyhead; or simpler still as a ticket to La Guardia Airport and a taxi to Fifth Avenue. A navigator at sea deals in terms of degrees (for direction) and degrees and minutes (for distances). Both degrees relate to the arc of a circle (think of it as a wedge cut from a round cake) and indicate the size of the angle at the centre and a point or a distance on the circumference.

So far as direction is concerned the circle is the circle of the modern 'degree' compass – more accurate than the old 32-point compass with its N, N by E, NNE, NE by N, NE and so on. Think of it as a clock face. This gives 0° as 12 o'clock or North, 90° as 3 o'clock or East, 180° as 6 o'clock or South, 270° as 9 o'clock or West, and with 360° we come back to noon or midnight or North.

Unless otherwise stated all the directions given are compass/magnetic. Compass bearings are affected by deviation and variation. Deviation is the effect on the compass of the iron structure of a ship and in a small wood or fibreglass yacht can be ignored. Variation is due to the difference between the true poles and the magnetic poles and is shown on all charts. On our voyage the difference was not very great except in the South Atlantic, where it reached 24°.

For dealing with distance, degrees and minutes are measured on the earth's surface. Any circle (called a 'great circle') that goes right round the earth, e.g. the Equator, is about 21,600 nautical miles long so that 1° (divide by the 360° of a circle) will be 60 miles and 1' (divide by 60) will be one mile. Distances North and South can be simply measured from the Equator 0° to the Poles 90°. Distances East and West are measured from the Greenwich Meridian 0° going East or West to the International Date Line 180°. This works out simply on the Equator, but the fact that lines of longitude gradually come together and join at the Poles causes a complication that has to be allowed for by calculation or using tables. As an example, supposing the Houses of Parliament are 51° 30' North and 0° 10' West, then they will be 3090 miles North of the Equator and about 8 miles from Greenwich Observatory, where 0° Longitude is shown by a brass strip. If you go to see it, you will find that it has been moved several times to get it in just the right place.

This note is not meant to teach navigation (you need a reliable book for that) but to make parts of the narrative more accessible.